D0113856

HQ
759
.T29
1992
Den

MOTHERING
HEIGHTS

RECLAIMING
MOTHERHOOD
FROM THE
EXPERTS

SONIA TAITZ

WILLIAM MORROW AND COMPANY, INC. / NEW YORK

WESTERN IOWA TECH - LIBRARY
87602

Copyright © 1992 by Sonia Taitz

All rights reserved. No part of this book may be reproduced or utilized in any form or by any means, electronic or mechanical, including photocopying, recording, or by any information storag or retrieval system, without permission in writing from the Publisher. Inquiries should be address to Permissions Department, William Morrow and Company, Inc., 1350 Avenue of the Americas, New York, N.Y. 10019.

It is the policy of William Morrow and Company, Inc., and its imprints and affiliates, recognizing the importance of preserving what has been written, to print the books we publish on acid-free paper, and we exert our best efforts to that end.

Library of Congress Cataloging-in-Publication Data

Taitz, Sonia.
    Mothering heights : reclaiming motherhood from the experts / Sonia Taitz.
        p. cm.
    ISBN 0-688-10588-2
    1. Motherhood—United States. 2. Parenting—United States.
I. Title.
HQ759.T29 1992
306.874'3—dc20

Printed in the United States of America

First Edition

1 2 3 4 5 6 7 8 9 10

BOOK DESIGN BY JAYE ZIMET

To Paul, who takes me there

ACKNOWLEDGMENTS

Many thanks to Lawrence Van Gelder of *The New York Times* for his early support for my journalism (likewise Mike Leahy and Connie Rosenblum); Penelope Green for her openness to quirky sensibilities (ditto Suzie Bolotin and Carol Kramer of the dearly defunct *7 Days*); Stephanie Wood of *Child* magazine, who does it with style and warmth (as do Freddi Greenberg and Carolyn P. Hagan); Superwoman Susan Ginsburg, my agent; soft-spoken, smart Susan Leon, my editor; and fellow parent-troupers Julie Stuckey, Pam Hogan, Adolfo Profumo, Peg Kolm, Hiroko Davidow, Anne L. Strassner, Kelly Kaminski, Cathy Hausman Kaminski, Melinda Marshall, Jean Rosen Cohen, Ann Wilson, Barbara Hiller, Simone Schloss, Debra Case-Tane, Marla and Wesley Strick, and Karen Pritzker.

Last, most of all—to the late Carol E. Rinzler, lawyer, editor, writer, and mother of two, who always cheered me on.

CONTENTS

INTRODUCTION:
SOME VIEWS
FROM
MOTHERING
HEIGHTS

Baby Boom I, meet Baby Boom II: There appears to be a new crowd in the communal wicker bassinet. Younger parents, as well as an affluent set of older parents, are having their requisite 2.2—and spending more and more on them. Over 4 million babies were born in the first fiscal year of the nineties, the largest number of little dividends since 1962. Marketers have not been oblivious to this fertile warming trend.

A recent *New York Times* article was entitled "It's a Boy! It's a Girl! It's Time to Shop!" This astute piece covered a toy fair, the iceberg tip of an industry worth approximately $2.5 billion. Among the heralded new products were diapers patterned like improbable animals, Nike-shaped infant carriers, and car-seat covers fashioned after the works of Jackson Pollock. It seems that new parenthood, of which I am a member, means bucks to a growing number of entrepreneurs.

It also means status, deserved or not, among a growing number of experts who seek to control parents' lives, and often succeed. Contemporary motherhood is an insatiable obsession, and often involves: The La Leche League breathing down your neck (or bosom) with demands that you breast-feed (or your poor baby will have no antibodies), baby masseuses who claim that unmassaged tots never quite "bond," catalogs crammed with brain-enhancing materials, and franchised exercise classes for the newborn.

Incidentally, there isn't an atom of truth to all this. I was raised watching TV, pre-Sesame TV, with a foreign-born, non–English-speaking grandma periodically spooning processed carbohydrates into my open, toothless mouth. By all rights, I should be retarded, and not just mentally. Somehow, I felt that I was not. Then, nearly four years ago, I became a mother, and something happened. A weird, throwback combination of fear, ignorance, boredom, and curiosity made me open (and toothless) to the processed carbs of experts. There seemed to be an endless supply of them, each with his own form of dubious nourishment. And I, and every mother I knew, seemed to have an endless hunger for it all.

Modern mother culture features much technical, unwanted, and personal advice for the parent: There are doctors who will recommend "trying" for a boy after a family has had a girl. They offer methods, pre- and post-conception, to assure this perfect family. There are psychiatrists who offer to watch and even videotape mother and child to see if they are doing all right in the critical bonding months. (Home visits, at a price, are also an option.)

There are toy clubs and "child development programs." There are classes to teach us which toys are more "educational" (whatever that means in the context of cooing babies), and there are classes that teach mothers to teach *other* mothers which toys to prefer, and buy. There are "parenting" seminars for the nervous (or lonely)—which hope to dictate your every move for a decade or so, and there are avalanches of primers, claiming that they (alone) will help you raise a happy, healthy, straight, and loving child.

Somehow, the roles women play—wife, lover, mother—continue to become traps of cost-effective cliché. In the fifties and sixties, wives were—*had* to be—pie bakers, martini makers, June Cleavers (named, perhaps, for her repressed anger). In the seventies or eighties, lovers were—*had* to be—multiorgasmic sexual athletes. The nineties demand that each mother be exemplary, birthing without pain (or drugs), bonding on the spot, loving without ambivalence.

Like those before it, this decade takes on the marketable subtleties of a private phenomenon: parenthood. Mothers are being teased out of the home and into the agora for a public trial. Are we doing it right? Do we have the right touch? The right toys? The right lights? Is our child going to grow up tall, thin, and bright? Something private, and precious, has become public, vulgarized—and scored by impersonal judges. What used to be ours has become theirs, again, under the spotlit microscope.

Pressured by a huge number of "experts," mothers, working or at home, may begin to buckle. Part-time mothers (an oxymoron if ever there was one) may surrender to their free-floating and always exploitable guilt by sending their kids to "enrichment" programs. They hope, or are told, that in doing so, they are doing all they can for their young child—who may otherwise have to spend the day with the cipher one has hired to raise him.

Full-time mothers have their buttons pushed, too. Many of them, having turned, or been turned, away from high-status careers, may be easily convinced to turn motherhood itself into a career of sorts. This career, as good as any man's, becomes a complicated, technical process, requiring training, special equipment, and an inspirational program from mentors up above.

It's really about power, isn't it? About easy experts, most of whom—surprise!—make heady profits from their supposed benevolence, telling you, the parent, that you need to buy this gadget, that opinion, their way of life. All can be taught, they say. Certainly, all can be bought: the rattle that will encourage your child's curiosity; the video that will make your child happy, never bored, and take him out of your hair, without guilt; the book that will teach him about kindness to animals, racial tolerance, and God; the book that will teach *you* how to see that child of yours as he or she really is.

Ah, but they can't teach you that. Through a series of gradual power losses, the modern parent is in danger of losing sight of her own child, as well as her own vision and style. It's a very big price to pay emotionally. Too bad it's often accompanied by an equally huge price financially.

There's a child born every minute; the sucker, increasingly, is you and me. What makes us suckers is our alienation from the opportunity right before our eyes. What makes us suckers is our fear of going by our instincts, alone. It's hard to do, and I certainly haven't got there.

Since my metamorphosis into "mother," I've been bombarded with information and misinformation about how to raise children, with the implicit threat that, failing to fork over some dough, I'd be lost in a modern wilderness not even Dr. Spock could hack through. So I have forked over.

Warily, hoping not to understimulate or deprive, I've bought the books, the tapes, the videos, the rattles. I've massaged, Gymboreed, and tried to ace the nonending course load. In the process, I've become part of an enormous mail-order chain letter encompassing mothers from coast to coast.

Here, for example, is my morning's mail, mostly unwanted: two toys ($18.65) from a reputable parents' magazine (these toys will keep coming until one of us—my infant son or myself—grows up and/or cancels); a brochure for sleep away camp (my oldest child is not yet four); a book club offering to teach the wonders of science to preschoolers; and (contradictorily?) an invitation to the Now You Can Read Bible Stories Book Club.

I have also received an envelope stuffed with "coupons and offers chosen especially for cost-conscious parents of preschool-age kids, as seen on TV!" These include "enormous savings" on film development; Gerber life insurance (!) "for the child you love . . . because children do grow up;" a special offer on ASA film; a special offer to "write children's books" from the "Institute of Children's Literature" (*Caveat Vendor:* I *am* sending for that revealing test for writing aptitude); a magnetic "Genius Maker," which is (disappointingly) a set of tinny boxes containing letters and numbers ("super-fun play!"); and "Give Your Child a Headstart: colorful non-toxic fun learning puzzles"—those super-fun letters and numbers again—that "lure your child from TV!" (except for ads promoting these coupons and offers, presumably).

There is also: "My School Years Keepsake & Memory Album," which "Takes Child from Pre-School to Prom Night," with nary a pause for the development of better taste; "The Time-Life Library of Curious and Unusual Facts" (example: "The Death-Defying Leap of Mark Mongollo"); an offer to have Baby's first shoes bronzed "forever"—*plus* you can "also save on portrait stands . . . bookends . . . and wall brackets . . . all beautifully designed and handcrafted to display your baby's first shoes"; and Elizabeth's Homecoming, the "First Issue in a Heartwarming Baby Doll Collection" (fifty-eight dollars will get you started on this).

And there is: "Mommy, they're playing *my* song"—Introducing eighteen minutes of personalized songs by "Michael"—are we supposed to have heard of this man?; a dozen personalized pencils and/or golf tees: "WOW! What a Great Value! 5 Books and 2 sets of flash cards," the latter featuring alphabet and numbers, from the Sesame Street Book Club (flash cards? *et tu,* Sesame?); *Sesame Street* magazine; Disney Presents 81 Favorite Children's Songs; Disney's Premiere Collection: 10 Read-Along Stories from Your Favorite Disney Movies; an offer from the Sears portrait studio; a discount coupon for Sofkins "bath tissue" for kids ("You're confident that your child is really clean!"); and, finally, a discount coupon for Rainbow Chips Deluxe (you're confident that your child is really sugar-shocked).

Most mothers have mailboxes stuffed like mine. Most pick up parents' papers and magazines, only to find endless ads for classes, shrinks, toys, tapes, "mother networks" and book clubs. Is it any wonder that parenthood is burning us out?

Recently, tapping the ashes, some instinct began to flare up. There I was, attending classes and seminars with the rest of the novices, buying everything and buying *into* everything, and there *it* was, my instinct. It told me that I was becoming less, not more, informed about the deep, intermingling splendor of children and their parents. That we mothers and fathers know more than we think we do—just as Dr. Spock tried to tell us—and that what we don't know, quite often, can never be taught.

No one denies that parenthood is, like love and death, one of the holy terrors of life. It is—as my first law professor said about my contracts paper—full of brilliance, nonsense, and mistake. It is full of pity, terror, shame, and boredom. But no one is going to actually get us through this. We have to go through this alone. We have to live this parent's life, the way we've lived through all that happened before the kids came. And the way we'll live through our lives when the kids grow up and away (yet are still somehow able to torture us).

Much that is urged on us new parents is useless, because we didn't really choose it. It was pushed on us. It—whether it be Raffi videos, French lessons, or the complete works of Brazelton—might be just right for you and your particular child. But it is only right when *you* feel that it is. You know your family best; you decide. You are, after all, the one with the clout: the caring guardian of your own child.

The best parents I know are untutored. They simply are singular people, people who, before they become parents, made art of existence itself. Most had traveled, some had switched careers, all were observant, amusing, and kind. (One of them, by the way, is my husband, who came to me from a small English village, via Oxford, and now—commendably—gets a kick out of New York City.) As parents, these people keep true, and they keep growing. They are original, sexual, self-searching, and self-knowing. Having kids, to them, is a welcome trip to sea—— storms, full fathoms five, and all.

They don't take what other people say too seriously. They're not too fussy about dust on the carpet or mismatched clothing or an infinitely variable child. They and their children find their own way, together. They author their own lives.

This book argues that having children should not signal an alienated, borrowed existence (for which we desperately need help). Let's not hand ourselves over to Big Brother expert, Big Mother seminar leader. By developing ourselves, our interests, and our instincts, we can reclaim motherhood.

Parents need to be human beings, instinctual, fallible, and happy. Yes, happy. What will our children remember of us, ten, fifteen years from now? The mobile we bought or didn't buy? Or the tone in our voices, the look in our eyes, the enthusiasm for life—and for them—that we felt? They, and we, will remember the spirit of things, not the letter. Those memories will go so deep that no one could measure it, capture it, bronze it, or put it in a scrapbook.

Parenting is an existential art, a form of Zen mastery. The proof of its success is your joy in it, which your child will acknowledge. An expertise in living is the greatest legacy you can leave. Be, don't study the handbooks. There are a million ways to raise a child. If you read a million books, you'll know all of them. But the one you won't know is your own way. Your child isn't in a book, a seminar, a TV show, and neither are you. Love emerges out of time and trial, and error.

There's an old Woody Allen joke about cheating on his philosophy exam by looking into the soul of the student sitting next to him. That's what we do when we look away from our children and our unique responses to them. We, and they, are unique, inimitable. Don't cheat the experience.

My own experiences are at the core of *Mothering Heights*. In it I weave through a maze of experts, and find a way back to my home. You will find your own. Do you remember the ending of *The Wizard of Oz?* Dorothy finds out that the wizard's a fraud. "Disregard that man behind the curtain," he booms into the mike, still conjuring the image of the great godlike guru he isn't. Where is the magic? In Dorothy's own two feet. They will get her back to Kansas. Yours will take you back to your own family, its truth and its beauty. Shod them in red and get going.

A WORD ABOUT OBSOLESCENCE: It occurred to me, early on, that in writing about infant massage classes, baby gyms, and even the great bearded Raffi, some of the phenomena would vanish, passing into the dimension where pet rocks float, unclaimed. If they do, so much the better; what was once considered a necessity for mothers, something to spend money and worry on, has found its rightful place in the whimsical limbo. That is also what this book is about.

Inchworm, inchworm
Measuring the marigolds
Seems to me
You'd stop and see
How beautiful they are.

—*Nursery rhyme*

MOTHERING
HEIGHTS

ONE

WHEREIN BABY IS JUST A GLEAM IN MAMA'S EYE

You have decided to start a family. You look at your honeyed one. He looks at you. You kind of still adore each other. There is hope for the future. You want to reproduce. A touch of divine madness. You click off the TV, engage the answering machine. You light a candle.

You start giggling, then go quiet. You get all serious. The room seems sort of dark and shadowy. You make a try at becoming pregnant. That's it, you begin to make love. For the first time, existentially, you really mean business.

STOP!!!

Enter the experts with a team of mops, brooms, bleach, and nagging propaganda.

What about your pre-prenatal health?

Have you been taking multivitamins and minerals for the last three months? Heavy-duty ones, that will ensure, positively guarantee, no birth defects, blue eyes, and entrance (early decision) to Princeton? Mmmmmm-hmmmmm.

All right. We experts on babies and all appertaining to babies (mothers, dads) have begun to say that it's already a *bit* late to start now (much worse, tomorrow), but better late than never. Probably. Dad, you could take a few multivitamins, too. Recent studies indicate that sperm, no less than eggs, are things capable of drastic mishandling. In any case, you'll help with the stress of pregnancy, labor, delivery, and college fees.

All right, the pair of you. As you were.

What's that? A glass of bubbly?

Are you *crazy?* What if you get pregnant? You won't know for the next few weeks, right? Are you going to keep drinking those nervous little nips of Mumm—how wrongly named—or are you going to straighten up and fly right? You're going to *be* a mum, you know. A *madre,* a mama, a Mom.

So drink some water. Yes, filtered; you never know what sickly pollutants and trace metals may have crept in there. And stub out that cigarette, ma'am. You *know* it's going to give you a low-birthweight baby with a low IQ and even lower ERBs (toddler IQ scores to you), who will never go Ivy or even to the safety school of your choice. If you live in New York and have no idea what ERBs are, stop right now and find out.

If not, continue whatever it was you two parents-to-be were doing. Come on: If you wait too long, your fertile period will be over until next month, and your eggs will age, ripen, and rot, and then you may have even more defects to cope with. So relax, but kind of hurry it along a little, too.

Hold it. Is that a pair of jockeys lying there on the floor, Dad? Lights on. Sit up a minute.

Honeyed one, someone had better tell you that if you want to make lots of nice fat babies, you have to wear boxers, that's right, loose baggy boxers, and I *hope* you did not enter the vicinity of any hot tubs lately, because lover, that's death to the entire sperm kingdom right there.

Right. You can lie down again.

The experts think everything's going to be just fine now, but you know, the whole thing's a mystery, so don't blame them if everything goes wrong. They're not God, you know. They grapple with chaos, just like you do. Or are about to do.

Speaking of God, did you two say you wanted a boy or a girl?

You haven't thought about it? Come on; the experts can help you there. There are new and improved ways to balance your incipient family, and praying for a boy's not one of them.

Please turn on the lights and take in some statistics, facts, and factoids, before you make an awful mistake and get the totally wrong-gendered baby for you and your lifestyle.

According to a growing number of experts, the sex of your child can and should be your choice. Did you know that more and more people, at younger and younger ages, are testing their amniotic fluid? They are also testing their chorionic villi, which is to say, having bits of their prenatal circulatory system removed for genetic analysis. Both amniocentesis and chorionic-villi tests, being invasive, carry risks to the fetus, but isn't it worth it to know if it's Sally or Sam?

It isn't? Okay. Technology is beginning to allow for sex-determining blood tests. A jab in the arm and you'll know. Those tests, of course, are intended to predict birth defects or their statistical likelihood, and are not for the shopping convenience, or worse, of restless parents. But then again, so were amnio and cv.

One prominent doctor complains that more and more of his patients are seeking out the perfect family, even if it means gender-based abortion (which he sorrowfully provides). For instance, they'll say that they already have a boy, so if this one's another boy (as determined by amnio or CV), forget the whole thing. It makes him ill to think about it—amniocentesis, for one, is done rather late in gestation (test around four months, results a couple of weeks later). He prays, he says, for the right results, and sometimes his prayers come true and sometimes they don't.

Some parents prefer using a process called sperm fractionation, during which semen is whirled, dividing yin from yang. Then only the male or female sperms are artificially inseminated into the womb. The only hitch is that fractionation reduces fertility, which could create a problem you didn't originally have.

You two crazy kids thought you could just make love without Doctor, did you?

Please plan ahead. Did you know, more and more people are deciding that they must have *both* boys and girls? Research indicates that families feel more complete with a child of each sex. You need girls, says the lore, because they're good for keeping you out of the cold when

WESTERN IOWA TECH - LIBRARY

you're old (remember that ditty: A daughter's a daughter the rest of your life). But you need boys, say the surveys, because they keep the marriage together in the first place. Men don't leave as often when there are baby men to raise. So try for one of each, preferably the male first, which is what still another survey says most families prefer. And don't try too many times: Dr. Joyce Brothers herself has said that smaller families do better—that is, divorce less often.

Most families try sex determination in the privacy of their own bedroom. They do it, literally, by the book. The best known of this genre is called *Choosing the Sex of Your Baby,* and it is an arguable but popular old chestnut by Landrum Shettles. Because of his innovative ideas about procreation, Dr. Shettles was in his day the *médecin terrible* of Columbia University. Now, perhaps ironically, he lives in Las Vegas, that center of wistful odds.

The Shettles method of boy-making favors the fertile period (typically mid–menstrual cycle). (There is now a watch on the market that will tell you—or rather, remind you, exactly when that is). It also involves the missionary position with deep penetration (*che macho!*), and a basic (rather than acidic) pH. Girl-making is a bit more tricky, since it involves actually avoiding the most fertile period yet still managing to get fertilized. (The watch tells you to do it two days before you ovulate). Perhaps as a result, fewer girls are born (100 to 106 boys), at least when parents and doctors do not intervene. The numbers even out later.

The numbers even out, partly, because boys are more apt to have certain genetic defects. That, of course, is why those early blood tests have been developed, but who's to stop experts—who's to stop us—from diving in with more preferences, demands, and worries? No one, that's who.

How rare that friend of mind, who—told by her doctor that her family of two boys really "needed" a girl and there were ways to get one—said, "I'm happy with what I have."

Well, don't think about it now. Sometimes during the last paragraph or so, despite all warnings, admonitions, the fact that you read too much and worry too much about what experts say (and worry's not good for your fertility), you did get pregnant.

You have got into the club.

Congratulations!

TWO

WHEREIN BABY IS JUST A BULGE IN MAMA'S TUM

I really don't want to worry you—worry's not good for your fetus—but wait. Hang on. *How* much weight did you say you've gained? Only three pounds in three months? As many as ten pounds in four? Too little—this year's goal is about 30–35 pounds. Too much—last year's was no more than 25. In any case, you'd better watch out and start analyzing what you may be doing wrong. It's good practice for being a modern mother. Try not to laugh—have you been touching that (poorly named) Mumm's again? I'm serious: not one drop!

You will need a sober head, for now your chores involve asking around, reading some books, and above all, moodily poring through magazines, newspapers, and veteran parents' lore for Troublesome Nagging Tidbits. (TNTs.) TNTs are carefully woven items, much like the booties of yesteryear, but they last much longer.

One TNT: a drop of Mumm's and your kid's in special school for life.

Another: Have you used a computer or a microwave lately? How about that electric blanket that some "friend" got you last Christmas? And that cellular phone?

Another: Did you know that flying takes you into a sphere of higher radiation? (Don't forget your husband's past airplane flights, before he inseminated you.)

Another: Remember that jogger who gained only twelve pounds and delivered a stillborn? That could be you. It's going to be you.

Another: Remember that mother who gained forty pounds and never lost it, so her husband left her sniffling in the tundra? That could be you. It's going to be you.

Another: Have you ever heard of gestational diabetes? Well, now you have, and if you get it, your child is going to be fat—gross—and her husband or his wife will leave him sniffling in the tundra.

Your doctor says everything's perfectly normal and you look great?

Hmmm. Better check and see if he's been sued for carelessness (or what lawyers call negligence). Is he overbooked? Did he really take a look at you? Some doctors are so busy, they really don't see what's under your paper gown, the way helpful friends, neighbors, magazine feature writers, and relatives do. Besides, most medical problems are subtle, invisible even—particularly those involving the unborn, who may or may not already have spina bifida.

Maybe you should get a second opinion. (Or a third, if you have already received the unsolicited advice of friend, neighbor, journalist, or relative.)

By the way, have you remembered to check the cesarean rate of both doctor and his or her hospital? There is still time to start worrying about that now. There is still time to find a midwife, not to mention the doula who will look after you when the baby is born (at home, while bread is baking), making sure that no one interferes with bonding in all five senses of the word.

If you are the worrying type prone to checking the cesarean rates of doctors and hospitals, though, perhaps you should find yourself a practitioner who takes lots of tests, warding off all sorts of tragically avoidable medical catastrophes.

Some very good doctors are known to take lots of tests and offer preview TNTs about conditions like that gestational diabetes, which you really might test for any time you visit, and pre-eclampsia, which could kill you and your child. Have you had any pounding headaches (not caused by ceaseless stress) lately? And have you heard about that virus that makes your child blind, deaf, and bad with numbers? No one knows how you can avoid catching it, but it can certainly interfere with bonding, though (now that you still have some time to yourself) you can read about it in several baby books. (It's called cytomegalovirus, not to be confused with toxoplasmosis, which is also everywhere, endemic, and ruinous.)

If you want to worry about your cats, you'll need to do extra research. Have you remembered to worry? Immediately start, for reasons A and B.

A. They will give you toxoplasmosis, which is heartbreaking. Everyone tells pregnant ladies this; it's got to be one of the most vital things they can be told. A friend of mind looked at me, looked at my huge, dumb cats, and said that my child would be born blind in at least one eye. (Tip: My child can see, but I no longer see the friend.)

How do you get infected with toxo-whatever? Well, it's very simple. All you have to do is eat raw beef or pork, or have a cat who's eaten same or worse—a rotten mouse. (Check the contents of those premium cans, ladies; first ingredient is select-grade mouse). The cat in the scenario then gets sick, drops a poop, and you ate it. Can't remember if you ate some cat poop? Time to start worrying in the doctor's waiting room, where the sight of all the other pregnant ladies will remind you that not every baby, statistically, can be born perfect, so if it's not them, sorry, it *has* to be you. (Goading your dread should be the TNT that states that toxoplasmosis can be carried by roaches or flies—so that you can get it even if you have no cat!)

B. Even if your doctor or midwife by *some slim chance* should deliver a healthy baby (of your choice genderwise, and with the right color hair, unblinded blue eyes, etc.), get rid of those animals. Don't you know they'll sit on your baby's face in the dark of the night and smother him or her?

C. (For extra credit) Don't you know that, according to a wonderful newspaper (for which I confess to have written), cat dander adds to the horrible consequences of dust, producing (together with dust or alone) an asthmatic condition in your child over the next ten years? It's a fact; the newspaper recently saw fit to devote quite a lot of space to the hazards of airborne particles, adding that dust itself can never be quite got rid of.

In fact, said these helpful recent stories, the death-by-dust problem is exacerbated, not helped, by vacuuming and shampooing. Newspapers, too, however elite, are full of bad chemicals. Do you happen to have any in your home, along with the dust? And have you seen the latest information about lead-laden soil, tracked into homes with every innocent footfall? It will leech I.Q. points from your growing family.

Don't clean your house *now;* you should be resting—otherwise your heart rate may go too high, and your body heat will rise and basically the fetal limb formation, which usually depends on your thinking about it all the time (like those planes you keep in the air with your fear), will go horribly awry.

You should be resting, and leafing through catalogs.

That is what pregnant women are supposed to do.

If you have not been sent any, don't despair. Just pick up one of those cards for a "free" subscription to any baby magazine (you can usually find them at any toy or child-furniture store). You will then discover what "free" really means. It means you have been forcibly taken into the circuit.

This circuit is more fertile than you. It will fill your mailbox forever and ever. When you remove it from the mailbox, you will find outstretched corporate arms, milking, milking.

THREE

WHEREIN BABY IS A DOLLAR IN THE MARKETER'S ACCOUNT

*T*his is sad. You thought that your child would be, at least at first, a relatively inexpensive venture. You would carry him or her on your broad maternal back, tied to you only by a well-worn rag (gingham). You would carry him into the wheat fields, lay him down to rest in a little box lined with warm towels.

Back home, you would find a fragrant drawer that you lovingly line with old blankets. You would lay him there, like a kitten (the breath-sucking, dander-full kitten you had to get rid of). When he grew a bit, your experienced sister lent you a crib with the regulation slat spaces and the regulation paint, nonlead. And when the gingham rag finally tore to shreds from loving overuse, your friend gave you a Snugli, which clearly indicates on the package that it will be perfect for toting baby till age four. (You also got rid of the rag shreds: choking hazard.)

You have since discovered that a baby-laden Snugli gets wearisome after the first five minutes or five blocks (whichever comes first). That is, unless baby is underweight, which is another debilitating worry, as well as cause for public shame and comment.

Digression on public shame and comment:

You have got to prepare for a lifetime of the pillory, for whatever you do will be seen as wrong by total strangers, up until and including the time when whatever your child does will be seen as wrong by total strangers. The latter condition is better, though, as your shame will be accompanied by a furious loyalty for your child, leading to stunning defenses—your head shouting through the pillory—of the kind you never thought up for yourself.

Speaking of shame, you do have some diapers—both cotton and cloth—for daily the controversy about the environment rages, and you will be screamed at for using a Pampers in a public place. You're not entirely sure whether it's worse to pollute the environment with plastic, urine, and poop or to use biodegradables, which some say don't degrade and in any case kill trees. You have read reports that perhaps cloth's the worst because it uses all that water and those phosphates, and because the trucks that cart the poop away stink worse than poop and permanently darken the air. And didn't you get that lovely letter from Pampers explaining how it was doing its best, and that reports of the earth's demise were greatly exaggerated? Your ease is also a factor; you are worried about having to change porous cotton cloths all day long in public places, for that, too, brings on shame, and fatigue.

Sigh (a shallow one, taking in little monoxide that could hurt fetus or quality/quantity of impending breast milk).

You have two infant chairs, one that bounces and one that rocks, and you've read that you must never, never leave baby in them unattended, and you intend to attend to those chairs, never taking your eyes off, not even to pee. (Although when you *do* finally pee, you will diligently Kegel, and if you do not know what Kegeling is, you will find out. Thus, you will regain sufficient tone to continue your marriage—for the child's stability—and even contemplate providing your only with a sib, thus teaching him or her to share and experience deep psychic pain.)

You have read that death comes quickly and often to carelessly parented children. You've read it in your special child-safety book that you bought when you bought Spock. The one that tells you that toilets, rugs, tables, stairs, walls, and even a common coin can kill your child. The pearls on your neck: *lethal.* Suppose one should fall off and Baby swallow it? The perfume behind your ear? Poison. Not the brand; the killer.

Oh, yes, and you have a car seat, an *infant* car seat, thank you very much, so that you can safely take your backward-facing baby home from the hospital, home to your lair of many hazards.

You got *nothin',* Mama.

Open the catalog(s) and open your purse.

Do you own or have access to:

- An assortment of black-and-white toys, not to mention the all-important downward-staring mobile? These are needed to stimulate baby's brain. Memorize the following equation: No mobile = No stimulation = *No brain.*
- An infant video? We will go into this in more detail in a later chapter. For now, suffice it to say that babies need not be deprived of hours by the television, mouths open in stupefaction, drool slowly making its way to the floor.
- Food mashers? Infant recipe books? *Petite* kitchen scales?
- Bottle warmers for home, car, and yard?
- A little crackly machine so that you can hear your baby wherever you are, as well as police signals and neighboring babies and their mothers?
- A wooden, early American–style high chair, practically an heirloom? (Who hasn't observed that fine tradition of placing baby's high chair, decades later, in its honored spot in the dining room?)
- Electric tush-wipe warmer? Buy one for every changing table in the house, and if you have not got more than one, get some.
- Subscriptions to child-development newletters that outline *exactly* what to do and when to do it, so that your child will see, hear, walk, and talk?
- Subscriptions to "developmental" toy clubs that come with vital "literature" on how to use them?
- Extensive safety equipment? More on this in the "Everything Can Kill Him" (and it's all your fault) section.
- Tapes that mimic the sound of the womb?
- Pillows that mimic the shape of the womb?
- Lamb throws that mimic the warmth of the womb?

- An extensive set of lullaby tapes that mimic the sound of a mother singing? (Perhaps as heard through a Prega-Phone when baby was still inside the womb? You say you aren't using a Prega-Phone to communicate with your fetus? Get one immediately and apologize—ideally, in a Romance language. If your accent is poor, borrow an au pair from the appropriate country and play Cyrano.)
- Transitional objects (stuffed animals to you) that mimic the friendly feeling that baby had in the womb, when you never disloyally stepped away from her? Be careful, though, that such transitional objects do not have button eyes, which can be awkward in the unlikely event that baby gouges and then attempts to devour them. (Recognize, in such a circumstance, that your child was trying to do that to *you*.)
- An intelligent swing, ideally that goes on forever, which mimics the feel of a mother rocking her child in her arms?
- Books that explain how to raise an exemplary child? More on this one later, too, but here's a rule of thumb: If your books, laid sideways, do not reach the height of your child, you have not got enough. Continue to purchase books until the numbers match.
- Books for your child's reading pleasure? Cloth, plastic, cardboard, and even—for the advanced (perhaps read to through Prega-Phone in the crucial first prenatal months)—a leatherbound *Britannica Junior*?
- Subscriptions to several children's "classic" book clubs?
- Huge toy boxes (with safety hinges), multicompartmented diaper bags, and miscellaneous fishnets to hold all your heaving paraphernalia?

Pick up the phone and drop a few thou. I'll wait.

Oh, the delivery's here already!

Okay, throw out the Styrofoam packing peanuts. Baby may choke on them.

Do not, however, forget to worry that thrown-away Styrofoam peanuts will pollute the planet and ruin your baby's longevity in that long-term, insidious way. Would it have been better to have let him nibble a few?

Force your mind away from planetary concerns—beyond the diaper dilemma, plastics, and insecticides. These may distract you from imminent danger in the home.

Examine the equipment you've bought. Check for structural defects.

Stare at the equipment, stare at your child, stare at the bills.

Feel overwhelmed.

Be even more overwhelmed when you realize that if you weren't before, you surely are now on every major mothers' mailing list in the country.

FOUR

WHEREIN BABY IS A CROWNING SPOT OF FUZZ IN THE OB'S EYE

Are you still pregnant? Isn't it, like, ten months or something? Have you actually forgotten to give birth? Pre-term babies may be small and light, and that's no good, but post-term babies are apt to suffer the effects of placental deterioration, and that's no good either.

So try to give birth exactly on time, not too soon, not too late. It's best not to tell people what your due date is, or they will nag you about it, trying, in some way, to *make* you do it. Some will urge you to eat hot Mexican food; others, to have sex; still others, to take a walk. All this advice is not only mutually exclusive, it is rude. It is best to heed the wisdom of no one.

Still, such wisdom has somehow been following you from the moment you began to "show." Strangers surrounded the fecund belly, grunt-

ing with tribal interest. It was as though you were Mia Farrow in
Rosemary's Baby. They had something urgent to tell you; there were no
words for it, just beams, grunts, and the occasional pat-pat-pat.

You tried to hide out, wear shades, wear a raincoat, but it was as
though you were suddenly famous. As rumored, fame brought no joy,
for as so commonly happens, it came from something you could hardly
take credit for (being female? copulating?). The life spark, you happen
to know, came from somewhere mysterious. That is the first real knowledge of parenthood, and you are still puzzling its awe as strangers give
you platitudes.

These platitudes, like your pregnancy, will grow and grow, reaching
a peak when baby actually arrives. Then, you will be told to put a blanket
on baby, to remove it, to give him sun, to shield him from sun, to pop
a pacifier in, to pluck it out. Still later, you will find Big Brother and
Sister touching your infant or child as they once touched you, and it will
feel as though they're *still* touching you, and they are.

You will be helpless. If you don't object, you will feel victimized
(the strong touch the weak, the big touch the small, and everyone loves
to touch delicate babies). If you do object, you run the risk of confronta-
tion with one hand tied (that is, with one hand clamped to the carriage).

Soon after my daughter was born, I was squeezing mangoes in the
outdoor market when I noticed that some man was bent over my baby's
carriage. He was tickling her nose. The germs, I thought, and the impu-
dence!

She, I noticed, was smiling, but that baby in the treetop might well
have smiled as the wind rockabyed her down.

"Don't think she likes that," I mumbled.

"Oh, yes, indeed, she quite does," said the man, looking up to
display a wide, round, yeasty face. Oddly, he was arguing about whether
the touch of rude men (with posh affectations) was enjoyable to my
infant.

"Look," I said—and then I flubbed a clever line a colleague with
the same problem had used. Frank, father of two small New York City
boys, had told me that he says, "Oh gosh, my baby's coming down with
something awful, and I don't want you to catch it!"

Adding my own twist, I ended up saying, "Babies easily catch
things."

Maybe I should have left out the brief lecture on pediatric immunology.

"BITCH!" said this friend of small children, turning quickly from Mister Rogers *manqué* to the matricidal Norman Bates. Negative allusion was then made to the orifice from which my little one first peered out at the world. "She'll always be unhappy!" he added, his moon mug darkening into a private hell.

Baby kept smiling, bless her. I checked as soon as I'd run down the street.

All this hoopla can be foretold by pregnancy itself.

At six months, I was informed, by a waiter in a rather nice resort, that I looked as though I were "about to burst."

Oh, come on, waiter: Do you think I'm going to order three courses now and tip you, too? We did tip him, actually, and well. Perhaps we realized that if I *did* burst, he could be helpful on the scene (wiping amniotic fluid, offering a mint, bringing plastic bags filled with ice chips, etc.).

If, however, you are exercising in the effort to avoid comments like that of the waiter, remember what the experts say about the body-heat limit. I think it's something like, if you've passed out from lack of fluids and hyperthermia, you've probably gone too far.

If you are not exercising, please remember to worry that you will be unfit for the trial of labor. (My Lamaze teacher said that giving birth was like running ten miles. Total lie. I've given birth twice and still take cars everywhere.)

Still, trial it is. You will be on trial for the following:

Did you use that chubby midwife who wears Birkenstocks or did you come to your senses and call Dr. Sleek back? (Okay, he's neurotic about pre-eclampsia and diabetes, he tests you every minute, and he's rumored to love the knife, but the babies are prettier that way, and he does throw in a tummy tuck for baby number two.)

No, really, did you pick the right person and venue for your birth? Midwife, nurse-midwife, birthing center, hospital, hospital birthing room, your own cozy sleigh bed? Have you contemplated the pros and cons of each? There are books that will explain that no woman should give birth without another female present, vigilant against internal or external fetal monitors, enemas, air-conditioning, forceps, and abbreviated bonding opportunities.

These books, should you choose to read them (others prefer knitting booties) will explain the medical horrors that hospitals have prepared for you. They will give you the score on all the people who are trying to hurt you, all the things that, years later, baby will remember having been done wrong (or unfeelingly). They will itemize all the indignities, the unwarranted procedures, the toxic chemicals, that are going to be poured into you by the *Medical Establishment*. (It's ironic that the person who wants everything "natural" and untrammeled will have gone around town researching every aspect of pregnancy, labor, and delivery, cross-examining thousands, and dreaming rare, detailed dreams about drugs and procedures no one but she and some neonatologist ever heard of.)

They will enlighten you about the value of private nurses and bring up the funny word "doula" again. For those of you who really haven't heard of doulas, they are like mother's helpers, except—I suspect, given the odd title—a tad more forbidding and humorless.

"YOU VILL NOT EAT ZAT HASENPFEFFER!!" yelled the doula.

Boiled down, these books will force you to confront issues of control, aesthetics, and the chance of injury or death for mother and/or child. Did you think you could just sit there singing "Sunrise, Sunset?"

Did you attend all your Lamaze classes, even that one on cesareans, which of course *you* (with those hips, and/or excellent choice of antivivisectionist M.D. or midwife) won't need? Are you retaining a lawyer in the event that your rights to vaginal delivery are infringed on? Your damage claim will center on the brute loss of bonding moments as they stitched you up, and of self-esteem—a loss cultivated by the myth that women who've had cesareans have not yet given birth.

Generally, in class, were you able to do that open-legged, head-to-the-ground thing? No excuse that you couldn't do it even when you were a virgin and fifteen. No excuse that you're now pregnant and listing toward forty.

When you breathe the "hee hee" breath, did your mouth form a faint smile as your instructor suggested, or did you look grimly determined? (Ask your husband.)

Did you actually release a faint oath as your husband pinched your arm in simulation of the labor contraction? (Lose additional points if the faint oath was released into a Prega-Phone.)

When your instructor began her brief digression into the available drug arsenal, did you *only then* begin to tune in and take notes? Did you listen when she added the deadly possible consequences of each drug? (If she didn't, your friends will supply the anecdotes—catheters lost in the brain, palsied children, crippled mothers.)

When she said that labor was like running ten miles, did you giggle sheepishly or skeptically? (Note-taking sans giggling is the right answer.)

Did you watch her tapes of real-life labor, alternately getting excited, tearful, nauseated, fearful?

Did you worry about whether the model for the above knows that such tapes of her private moments are bandied about à la Rob Lowe?

Did you try to reassure your husband that despite all appearances and the expletives you might perchance hurl at him *in medias res,* you will still be an attractive woman *inside,* and deeply, deeply still in girlish love?

Did you secretly wonder—despite your Lamaze instructor's ungallant demonstration of graphic drawings and gynecological videos à la Rob Lowe—about what ten centimeters of dilation actually looks like to a former bedmate? (And did you fear that strangers would impolitely dwell on this aspect of you as you later squeezed mangoes in the market?)

After the graphic instruction on pushing, did you wonder whether it was politically and/or sexually correct—by the standards of decades fifty through ninety—to defecate in front of a loved one, as the instructor said you might?

Did you believe the loved one when he said, after class, that on *you,* it would be attractive?

We're grown-ups now; let's not be coy: Are you planning to do your labor *au naturel,* or are you going to wimp out and take all the drugs they can cram into you?

Don't answer that one. You don't know yet. The trial of labor, like the trial of motherhood itself (and like death), must be experienced to be known. Each one is different, so different that I have wondered why women didn't invent different words for each station of childbearing, as the Eskimos reputedly have done for each aspect of snow.

For instance, there would be a word for the agony of the bouncing cab. Another for the one that makes you curse at your doctor but not your husband. Or vice versa. I suspect that these words have not been invented because no woman wants her tale contracted (pardon the pun) into a simple code word. We want shaggy dogs here, mariners' rimes; we want war stories.

So, above all, did you remember to ask each and every labor veteran (mother) to give you bloody tales of what befell her on that table?

I need no encouragement: Here are mine.

FIVE

WHEREIN BABY IS DUE ON A PUBLIC HOLIDAY

My daughter's due date was the Fourth of July, an exciting flashback to Colonial history. Since I am American and my husband English, it is obvious that she was expressing some sort of vote against once and future monarchic repression. As we have come to know Emma, we have learned that she is against repression of any kind, not only monarchic but parental, but that is a different mariner's rime.

From books, my doctor, and numerous birth veterans, I knew that few children arrive on their due date. So I had assumed that in my case, Emma would arrive a day or so, perhaps even a week or so, later. (Possibly checking in on Bastille Day, leaving doubts, given our fancies, as to her paternity.)

Ruminant, calm, I made plans for the Fourth of July, plans not involving doulas. My plans involved watching *The Good Earth* on the evening of the third and eating hot dogs on the Fourth. I expected that my plans would be uninterrupted by chaos. Would chaos dare descend on Mothering Heights?

I do know a woman, an OB/gyn, who planned to have girls only, and she did. She also planned their birthdays (giving all those daughters the same one). She got the cesareans she wanted, on the day she wanted.

Oh yes, some women want cesareans. They swear by them—no more fuss than a face-lift! That way, as one doctor pointed out, they can keep their travel plans, and Doctor can keep his. I think he was being facetious, for there is something to be said for a baby deciding when and how he would like to reveal his corporeal form. Something that supersedes that trip to Tortola.

In the case of the fecund female doctor with the same-birthday girls, only one thing went wrong with her plans. *Should* women invent a vocabulary for different birth stations, they will have to include the one in which—despite the most careful planning—your anesthesiologist messes up and you get a spinal headache, a severe throb-job that throws plans out of orbit for about three days.

Still, I resolved to have an epidural, human error or no.

I had listened to every lecture of my Lamaze instructor. I had heard the countless horror stories (delivery brings with it a sort of amnesia, making a certain Homeric embellishment necessary). I had planned this epidural from Day One. Lamaze or no Lamaze, nose to the floor or no, childbearing hips or no, ALL THE DRUGS THEY CAN CRAM INTO ME was my motto.

It was my motto even after watching *The Good Earth,* in which drugless O-Lan births Baby in the rice paddy, barely pausing between field work and cooking a hot dinner. With nary a squawk, girls.

DRUGS was my motto right until the Fourth of July, when my daughter *did* decide to enter the world. Clever girl, to arrive on her due date, beginning to rap on the wall sometime around midnight. Fireworks pounding the sky, lights flashing, rivers West and East quivering with thunder, and something popping in my lower abdomen.

There are, however, some not so clever aspects about the Fourth of July. It is not the best day on which to give birth, particularly if you wish to have that birth accompanied by the benefits of the epidural.

First, your doctor is apt to be barbecuing, or preparing to barbecue, his T-bone. As it was midnight, mine was dreaming (of T-bones), one hundred miles away, in the little town of Litchfield, Connecticut. The man, whom I am still fond of, did not seem to want to hear from me. Dedicated OB though he was, he was not completely convinced that he wanted to hear from my fetus, either.

He told me, rather dully, that there is such a thing as false labor. Of course I—who should be considered for an honorary OB/gyn—knew that! That's the one that—if you take a nice slug of Mumm's—goes away. Well, I'd done that (perhaps jeopardizing one IQ point, to be recouped with black-white mobile later). My labor had still tested true.

Then he told me that first children tend to come late, not on their due date. Dislikably, I insisted that I knew that, too, but that this first baby seemed not only punctual, but increasingly insistent on the punctuality of her groggy OB.

Suddenly, my water was breaking, my belly was aching like a million stomach viruses accompanied by the parting of the Red Sea, and I was short on words. These facts—that last rare phenomenon in particular—began to countermand the doctor's groggy hunch.

I added that the contractions seemed to be coming every five minutes. No, every three.

Doctor suddenly said that he was starting out for New York. He added that I might start getting ready for the hospital. 'Nuff said. The bag had been packed since, oh, March. What was it the Lamaze instructor said you had to have?

Lozenges (sugarless) for your parched throat, ChapStick for your cracked lips, tennis balls for back labor, Evian spray (pre-Chernobyl vintage) for your poor, burning face, socks for your blue, freezing feet, picture of amber waves of grain to stare at (focal point), rhapsodic music on the Walkman (auditory point?), sandwich for the husband, champagne for the two of you, camera, film, cannabis (just kidding, Officer).

We forgot the camera. We had removed it, recently, to photograph my huge, beautiful bump—that is, my full-bodied profile—and had forgotten to return it to its place. But we did not know this until it was too late.

It was very exciting. This was *it*. Deep down, I was thrilled to be having a child who was clever enough to come out on her interesting due date (for I figured that, with pains every three minutes, she might defy first-born lore—you know, the three-day labor with sweat-knotted hair and hollow eyes—and be born within twenty-four hours).

I was so happy, pains notwithstanding, that I took a shower, shaved my legs (a common mania, I hear), and looked into the mirror at my own surprised face. Though I was metamorphosing from the Dark Lady of the sonnets into something more maternal and pastel, I was still, somehow, me.

My cabbie did not seem to care that he was transporting a contracting uterus to the hospital. He drove over and into every pothole between my house and the hospital. He did not respond with sympathy or even interest when my husband, stricken, realized he had left the stupid camera behind. I got revenge, though: I leaked amniotic fluid on the seat. A trespass of ordinary civility? Yes, but I was in New York, I was in labor, and the fluid was colorless (free of the dreaded meconium).

Six hours later, Emma was staring at me with most curious blue eyes.

In the interim, I had not received my indispensable epidural. My OB got stuck (he *says*) on the highway, and without him, no one could administer the analgesic. So I did it *au naturel,* and didn't I crow.

To paraphrase Gloria Steinem, if men could give birth, they would brag about it the way I am bragging. Emma's cord was tied around her waist, making her yo-yo up and down for a record four hours as I futilely heaved. The urge to push, said to be irresistible, was in my case nonexistent. If anything, I had a strong urge *not* to push. I had an urge to check out, in every sense of the word. Check out of the hospital, into Tortola—or the world beyond pain and care.

Dr. OB had to use forceps, which are like salad tongs, placed precisely where you are in the mood to accept no more visitors. Did I scream? No. Did I curse? No. I was a bloody angel.

It's odd. My incredibly nice husband tells me I was sweeter than I usually am, which is easy. I was certainly more demure. All I said was a periodic "Someone please help me," in a voice so wan that no one seemed to mind, nor did I seem to expect them to. This is something, I realized, that you have to do by yourself—like hurtling down Killington. Disregard all those masked people; they are illusions. You are as alone as the dying and dead.

A hero, I tell you. I was proud, and elated, and about a minute after giving birth, I was saying, *Say,* who needs epidurals, anyway?

But the second time around, just so you know what hypocrisy does spew from the labor table, I certainly did have that magic needle. Contrary to popular belief, second babies don't always come more quickly than their elders, though mine, like his sister, came on his due date: June 4. Clever boy.

This time, there were no fireworks, no breaking of waters, no feeling of something wildly unleashed. Just a vast series of irregular contractions, some close together, some not, some merely achy, some worse than achy. For hours and hours, this was all I got. A slow parade, with a couple of tin whistles and the occasional flat-handed bang on the drum.

Finally, on a hunch, I lurched to the hospital, checked in, and had a nurse tell me to go get lunch. Lunch, as I knew from reading every book on the subject, would have to be something like Jell-O followed by broth, or broth followed by Jell-O. (New wisdom—oxymoron—is saying that you can eat whatever you want.) It was a hot and lazy day. We were in a coffee shop two blocks from the delivery room.

My husband, still in his everyday mode, excused himself and went to the phone booth in the back to make some calls to Tokyo, Hong Kong, places like that. He was manfully discussing foreign exchange with the Far East, when I suddenly felt that we had to rush back to the hospital. No, make that shuffle. I suddenly imagined that I could hardly walk.

I was glad with the drama of it all, though.

Less glad when Paul—who thought I was biding my time—did not return from the phone booth. My frantic wavings did not summon him from the back of the shop; they merely earned me another bunch of Jell-O cubes from the Greek waiter. Finally, my husband emerged, and I gave him the meaningful look that Lucy gave Desi, the look that said, "Honey, little Ricky's on his way."

But when I asked the admitting doctor how I was doing *now*, he shrugged. I wasn't used to this. I wanted the precipitousness of Emma's birth. A few hours later, we were still gently stagnant. I lay there, waiting, my husband sitting at the foot of the narrow bed.

We waited in that room full of fetal heartbeats, the most dramatic, subterranean sound on earth. Each bed—really a gurney—was separated from its neighbor by only a drab set of curtains. The heartbeats were rapid, insistent; they chased each other; they knew what they were doing.

Above this obstinate line of music I could hear several types of wondering sounds. Groans. Soft crying. A piercing wail from an adolescent female. One woman started shrieking, then abruptly stopped. I began to do my own first-stage breathing.

For those of you who have not yet given birth, I don't mean to scare you. It's really not so bad.

(For those of you who have, sorry about that huge fib.)

My doctor came in to have a look at me, and he told me that he'd check again in an hour. An hour later, I asked him if I'd be out within the day. He said, maybe, maybe not.

I wanted to be out within the day.

He suggested breaking my waters. After a quick confab, in which I determined that this was not an awful thing to do (to my child), I said, Please do.

We went up, finally, to the birthing room. Using what can best be described as an industrial-strength crochet hook, my doctor tried and tried to break my amniotic sac. It was hard going. He seemed surprised. It didn't feel too special on my end, either. Finally, he succeeded, and a warm trickle of fluid began to run.

The point of no return. The release of oxytocin, now known to be the sexual hormone, released at orgasm for both men and women, but the maternal hormone as well. A point to ponder, but not on the labor table.

A point to ponder sudden, horrible contractions.

I tried to remember if it had been so horrible the last time. So horrible that I thought it must all be some huge but claustrophobic, existenial joke. I suppose it was. I'm not sure. But I was sure, at that moment, that nothing could be more horrible (except emotional pain, another story entirely).

A friend had told me that during her own hard labor, she'd yelled at her doctor, "I'm paying you three thousand friggin' dollars, and if I tell you to cut my throat, cut my throat!" Suddenly, her line didn't seem unnecessary. But I did not want my throat cut, only an epidural.

Those of you who have given birth with midwives, or plan to, are probably smirking, analyzing, perhaps correctly, that Doctor's intervention (water-breaking) caused these precipitous pains, the consequent wish for an epidural. I maintain that we'd have got to that point eventually. In any case, I didn't and don't care, because I suddenly realized—a Eureka! experience—that I would have a new experience that day. A new labor, a different one. A new and different war story. All that, plus the cessation (or abatement) of pain. I was getting happy.

Hurriedly, I asked my doctor to inform me about the downside of the epidural. He was not too alarming. He also informed me that the best anesthesiologist in the hospital—not available on the Fourth of July—was on call at that moment.

Prone, I scrawled on my informed consent form. Then, curling my back like a Halloween cat, I held my breath and received the blessed shot.

Prior to that moment, I had looked at the monitor and seen contractions that had numbers like 80, 90. These were killers, the sorts of highs that in bad movies threaten to explode the torture meter, to burst the mercury.

Shortly after the epidural, I noticed that the contractions were at about 100. I felt only the merest tug. I laughed, yes, laughed, at my contractions.

That was phenomenal, and I began to understand the why and how of modern science. Vanquished by awe, I believe I even dozed a bit. Got my strength up for the pushing part, which—as you recall—ended up in Forcepsland the last time.

The pushes, too, came quickly, without forceps, without episiotomy (so there, Birkenstocks brigade). I felt the urge to push, I followed the urge. I felt good at this birthing thing.

Pretty soon, everyone in the room was yelling "It's a boy!" And it was Gabriel.

I felt uncommonly well. Our son didn't look too bad, either. I looked at him for a long, long time, choked back a sob, and then nursed him.

It's alarming how quickly you want to do it again.

SIX

WHEREIN BABY IS A BOOKING IN THE FILOFAX

When new mothers talk about nursing, quite often they mean breast-feeding. But sometimes they are also referring to the acquisition, for a time, of a professional baby nurse. This is a luxury, like military school or braces, with a similar goal of straightening out your life, and often the concomitant pain.

When Emma was born, we hired a baby nurse on the recommendation of a friend. Remember that your friend is not interchangeable with you at any time, and that goes double for the way you both are as parents.

When I turned into a parent, I experienced a real and total personality change that slowly shifted back to the "normal" me, yet has not completely vanished. I believe the two levels are now superimposed, with an additional sprinkling of mortality intimations.

One aspect of these major changes was the sudden need to depend on the kindness of friends, strangers, anyone who could help me approach the abyss of Motherhood.

It was not that Emma was so small and fragile. It was that I was, suddenly, so small and fragile. Insecure and many-thumbed, and a middling lactator to boot.

Minerva entered out lives with a flourish. Minerva was a Trinidadian nurse. Retained by a large and famous New York agency, she had worked with the sick and the dying, and with new babies of every stripe.

She was not our first nurse, really. The first was called Suzette. Suzette came with valedictory references: She will remake your life. She will become a member of the family (*another* one?) She will be your right arm, etc., etc.

Suzette sounded sweet, if a bit reserved, on the phone. (Obviously, you can't be that reserved if you make your odd living by going into people's houses at a crazy time and staying with them for weeks and weeks, hairnet and all.) When, however, Suzette discovered that we had a pair of cats, furry, incontinent and stupid, she quietly refused to continue the conversation. Like most phobics, she said she was allergic. Thankfully, she did not add to our problems by telling us that they could asphyxiate our child.

So Minerva was tapped to be the new new member of our family. When I called Minerva from my hospital pallet, the first thing I said was, do you like cats? Minerva laughed easily. "How many you got?"

She had a swinging, sophisticated laugh. She made the whole thing stylish, breezy. I imagined her taking our baby out on Fifth Avenue in a dark, capacious pram (except that we didn't live on Fifth or have a pram). I imagined her white uniform, especially those thick-soled shoes that would noiselessly take her here and there, sort of like the whitewalls on a Rolls. I also imagined the *efficient* Minerva. I imagined her applying cold compresses to everyone in our house, not excluding my glowing, crowing mother.

You wonder why nurses are needed when *grandmères* abound? My mother, who is, I think, typical, could scarcely remember how the whole thing went (though time and again she told me it went like lightning, and I should enjoy it). Besides, hospitals are different, recovery is different, diapers are different; the entire paraphernalia is different.

In my mother's day, one lingered in a twilight haze during delivery, lazed around for a week at New York Hospital, gazing moodily at the East River. One never, ever cut the cord, fried the afterbirth with zucchini, or bonded—whatever that was—on the table. Nor was anyone in a hurry to buy black-and-white mobiles or subliminally or liminally instructional bumpers.

My mother had not nursed me; it was considered a bit rad in those days, like being a lesbian, a vegetarian, or a socialist. So neither of us had any experience in that area.

As I was giving Minerva instructions about how to get to our apartment on the non–Fifth Avenue side of town, she cut me off with the comment that she did not need directions, a limo would be sent. A moment later, I realized that we would be the limo-senders. And I said, sure, no problem. For I was cowed.

It is extremely cowing, no pun intended and odd locution deliberate, to sit in a hospital bed with your newborn and try to take care of her for the first time. Newborns are tiny; their cry is loud; their discomfort, unfathomable; their limbs, limp, their huge heads, venerable and weighty.

They seem, on some level, to know just how to be themselves, a skill rarely found in new mothers. They know what they want and what they don't want.

Mine didn't seem to go in hugely for the breast-feeding bit. With Minerva on the phone, in one hand, and my nipple in the other, guiding it into my daughter's screaming rosebud mouth, surrendering on the limo issue seemed the only way to go.

We, on the other hand took the common yellow taxi home from the hospital. We remembered, of course, to put our daughter in the middle of the backseat, strapped into her car seat, even though she fell right to the bottom of it in a saggy heap. We had been warned by our Lamaze instructor that it would be stupid to go through all that hard labor and delivery, only to have your baby get hurt in a car crash. (Since then, I have rarely, if ever, seen a New York mother haul a car seat into a cab for routine trips. Not only would the cabbie kill you—both of you—for the delay, but most cabs have no back seat belts, and hauling that item around during the course of your otherwise pedestrian day—along with baby, baby bag, and baby carriage—is nigh impossible.)

At any rate, Minerva arrived fresh. We arrived haggard.

She wore glamorous shades, which she removed to reveal glamorous, knowing eyes. We had no eyewear to protect us. We looked tired; we were tired. We could hardly see to see.

Consider that the metaphor for the rest of this section.

SEVEN

WHEREIN MOTHER IS A DUD IN HER OWN HOME

inerva was great with the baby. She held her easily—Emma's body seemed to leap into her arms like an accomplished ballerina with a fabulous partner. Though she periodically terrified us with her wails and her kicks, she did not terrify Minerva, who merely chuckled.

I liked the woman for the way she sized things up, gave them a name, and kept cool. More than cool. And I liked her for liking Emma's "style," as she called it. She started pointing the style out to us.

"Look at the way she's crossing her legs. Like she's lying on a beach chair."

"Look at that—she's joking with me. You jokin' with me, Emma?"

She seemed genuinely excited about our baby. Her excitement trained our eye to subtleties. It was like first contemplating the bust of Homer with an art historian, a professional bust-contemplator. And Minerva was on the ball. The things she picked up in Emma, the energy, the fun, the fire, are all still there. It was wonderful to be able to rhapsodize over a person with another person, without either getting jealous or bored.

But.

She was the first person to label our child as having a "little temper," and this label stuck around for too long. T. Berry Brazelton (love that "Berry") has warned parents about such labeling in his book *The Earliest Relationship* (cowritten with Dr. Gerard Cramer), but I was unable to read it until two years later. Often, this sort of "helpful" commentary is a projection of the name-caller's own emotional matrix. Minerva herself, that is, may have preferred more docile beings—perhaps that is why she never worked with anyone over the age of three months. At the time, however, I took her comment at face value, and it ultimately made me fear poor Emma more than anyone should have.

And: A nurse in the home is a grossly inhibitory presence. Bad enough a stranger—this is a stranger in a white uniform, a stranger in a white uniform who visits when you are somewhat indisposed, and peers around a *lot*. Our reaction, I think inevitably, was to feel disempowered. This was true even though Minerva was not one of those nurses, spoken about with either reverence or loathing, who come into your house and tell you what to do. The type that grow haughtily insulted if you question them, because, after all, they are doing what they are trained to do, and you, Mother dear, are not. Minerva was much too easygoing and confident to play that game.

We were disempowered merely by the presence of an "expert" in the home. Every time we wanted to figure something out, we asked her. That process, asking her instead of figuring it out ourselves, or simple trial and error (not to mention trial and success), led us to take all her opinions for granted, from the medical to the folkloric.

"Girl takes after her father's looks; gonna be lucky."

Well, that wasn't so bad. Still, I did want Emma to look like me a little. (Possibly to dispel the "temper" myth via homey familiarity.) Doesn't she, Minerva, at least around the cheeks?

"Doesn't she what?"

"You know, um, look like me? At least around the cheeks?"

People were always misled about whom babies resembled, I thought. They always went by coloring. Both Emma and my husband were blond and blue-eyed.

"Look like *you*? No, uh-uh."

Then there was the motherly commentary.

"You look tired, lie down."

"But can't I walk around a little?"

"No. You should rest."

"Get the blood going?"

"No, uh-uh."

Now we all know that enforced rest is delicious. But then comes the Gulag stage. Without a nurse to tell you to rest, you might just get up and look around to check if everything is the way it used to be before you gave birth. (It isn't.) Then you can rearrange it in a feeble attempt to feel safe in your new scary life. But no: In the Gulag, you are told, once again, to put your feet up.

It is also hard to cry around a stranger in your home, nurse or not, look like hell (i.e., like postpartum motherhood), wail to your husband, or drop large black clots of blood. At least it was for me.

Minerva seemed attuned to the glamorous and not to large black clots of blood. She read *Cosmo* and the biography of Jessica Savitch, who, though doomed, always had neatly groomed hair and no problem, from what I could surmise, with her figure. And there was I, plodding barefoot, dripping, oozing, groaning, and—worst of all—hospitably smiling.

Minerva rhapsodized about having worked with the rich, the famous, the dwellers on Fifth Avenue. Women who tended to favor the scheduled cesarean plus tummy tuck, and bled little during or after either. Paul and I listened to her tales of the immortals, we of the fuzzy-wuzzy, lived-in West Side flat. Except for having coincided on the Sending of the Limo ritual, our culture and the one she described seemed somehow different.

Of course we also had a baby nurse in common, although we "kept" ours, as they say, for two weeks instead of the East Side half-year. But every day we thought about what it was costing and swallowed enormous groans.

The worst of this borrowed, improbable luxury is that it's addictive. Someone is there in case of the always-possible-awful. *Someone else seemed to be responsible:* That is comfort akin to a narcotic (which on rough days I dreamed of taking).

That is why, when our second baby was born, we employed a nurse again.

We did not employ Minerva again.

We did not hire Minerva again almost entirely because of the *breast-feeding problem,* which deserves a chapter of its own. One hint: The Fifth Avenues had not placed great stock in breast-feeding; nor did Minerva.

We hired Nicole, who was recommended to us by a friend of a friend of a friend. She was reputed to be incredibly warm, impossible to exhaust. She was also reputed to be a veritable whiz at the arcana of breast-feeding, as mysterious and variable in its way (positions, length, quantity, mutual satisfaction) as sex, and quite often the rival of same.

EIGHT

WHEREIN BABY IS A TIPPLER AT THE BREAST

*D*ue to a persistent and unmistakable protest from my first child, I had hardly breast-fed her. After six weeks laden with tears, bottles, and a trickle of mother's milk, I had stopped trying.

I did a better job with my second: three-and-a-half months (that extra fortnight means something to me), with a complementary bottle or so a day. Why I succeeded with one child and not the other is a puzzlement, as is the fact that most women ascribe concepts like success and failure to the act of nursing. (In England, interestingly, the term "nursing" refers to the holding of a child, a dry but affectionate act that can be performed by parents of either sex.)

The mysterious variables of lactation, however, are so complex, so ineffable, that I believe it's a miracle whenever all goes well. What makes all go well? A calm baby, a calm mother, supportive folks all around, the absence of mockery, good nutrition, lots and lots of water, and luck.

Some people swear by the La Leche League, a national organization of volunteers who swear by breast-feeding. According to them, only the breast-fed are happy and secure, can hear properly, have straight teeth, etc., etc.

My doctors seem to think that since the disease differential between breast and bottle babies is negligible, the main advantage of breast-feeding lies in the lesser transmission of food allergies—if allergies run in the family—a push in the direction of intestinal development, as well as some maternal gratification.

Not only do the Leches want you to get that maternal gratification, they want you to get it everywhere, anywhere, exclusively, forever, and even if you have had a wiggly, recalcitrant, and nonsuckling sort of child. To further that end, they will stop at nothing, counseling that the baby sleep in the bed with Mother and Dad, be nursed well into the toddler years, and even be nursed if premature (despite having been bottle-fed for the first few weeks) or—get this—adopted. They take quite seriously a gadget that is basically a straw taped onto the breast, so no excuses if you have little or no milk.

Theoretically, this device should mean that men can now breast-feed, but the Leches have not, to my knowledge, pushed that idea. I think the doting grandparents—male and female—might just pick that up and run with it.

My daughter was distinctly of the nonsuckling creed. I don't think she would have suckled even at that straw-taped-to-the-breast gadget. But since I had bought the breast-is-best package (part of the give-your-kid-the-edge package), my short story was fated to grow longer.

I got the League's stout, sober book about nursing and studied it. Hmmm. No bottles at all, anywhere. *Nada.* But my hospital had given Emma water, *sugar* water. Ooops.

Then I read about total-demand feeding. Feed your child any time she asks, for as long as she wants. But she was hungry every minute; it took ages to feed her; by the time I fed her (since I was in the one-drop-per-hour category), she'd be hungry again (and breast milk is digested quickly). I felt I ought to and would drop dead, and make this whole thing moot.

Much of this whole thing has nothing to do with the health of babies. It has more to do with the image of motherhood, of women's bodies. And, as with most things that involve motherhood and women's bodies (birth control, abortion), breast-feeding is political.

The glowing, hazy photograph on the cover of the La Leche book is one clue. The title, *The Womanly Art of Breastfeeding,* is another. We have entered a creepy world, and the cost of admission is a simple, mammalian fact: We are the breasted half of the childbearing pair. The iconography machine goes mad, churning out Hallmark sentiments. Standing at the threshold of a new identity, I am reminded of the little pamphlets we got in junior high that sang out the pretty wonders of "Your Menses." (Yes, *your* menses, like your sorority, your cruise director, your League, La Leche, with its clubby, Esperantist sound.)

Underneath this Tipper Gore and Tupperware mentality lurks something dangerously similar to those old fifties notions (and everything old is new again) that rammed biological imperatives up women's wombs.

Once, we were told, have children; you were made for them. Don't use birth control, don't terminate, don't shirk. You have a womb; use it often and well. La Leche and its followers say essentially the same thing about your heaving, milk-filled breasts. To waste a drop would be unmotherly, unwomanly, *unnatural* (you mean, like the Pill?).

I was a humble new mother who, still bloodily draped on the delivery table, obeyed the new dictate that infants should be taken immediately to the breast, lest bonding be severed with dire health and emotional consequences. Though all my limbs were shaky, I managed to offer my precious few droplets of milk (actually, it's colostrum) to a bemused baby girl as watchful, masked nurses nodded approval all around. For six valiant weeks I tried—we tried—to eke out an infant's daily three squares. (In breast-feeding terms, it's really ten squares or so; the downside of the stuff's famous digestibility is an infant who is hungry day and night.)

Emma wriggled and screamed. She grew red in the face. She looked betrayed. She lost weight—damning proof of something unmotherly afoot.

Now some mothers would not stop nursing at this point. They would keep trying until they got it right. I know a woman who right now is nursing a six-month-old baby every hour, day and night. He is rather small, allergic to most things, and sleeps in the family bed, but she refuses to quit. "He'll thank me later" seems at the bottom of this, but I am dubious about that.

Minerva was with me when we took Emma to the doctor for her one-month checkup. The doctor didn't seem too worried. When I asked him what I could do to improve the breast-feeding, he told me to get more rest. Minerva mumbled to herself, "Kid's starvin.'"

Back home, I asked Minerva if she thought my milk would kick in after a while. You know, if I rested more.

"No, uh-uh."

Why not?

"Here, let me try something."

"Something" meant a bottle.

I was caught between the Leches and Minerva.

I tried to explain the maxims of breast-feeding to my nurse (misno-mered): Bottles cause conflict, nipple confusion (baby's), nipple neglect (mother's), and a gradual loss of milk.

Minerva listened to my brief lecture. She stared at my swollen Jayne Mansfields and bewildered demeanor. She wanted to be kind. She paused, formula bottle in one hand. And then she gave me her own best maxim:

"Just because you're stacked doesn't mean there's anything in those balloons."

The next sound I heard was the sound of Emma sucking at the bottle to her heart's content. It was an audible squeak. When I left the room, both my eyes and breasts were uselessly dripping, one set more than the other.

I was goaded further by another lactating acquaintance. This one had a large and strapping child. Like a milk archer, a two-breasted Ama-zon, the woman boasted about how much and how far she could "shoot." She was being macho (or femmo), but she got to me. I picked up the phone and called the League.

Holy cow. An intimately hushed voice, the voice of bereavement experts, midnight FM jockeys, and phone sex pals (this call was free) took over my life. It laid down the La Leche Law so that I could not ever forget it. I will paraphrase:

> YOU MAY NEVER, EVER USE A BOTTLE, NOT EVEN
> IF YOUR NEWBORN SCREAMS, STARVES, AND REVERSES
> ONTOGENY AND PHYLOGENY TO BECOME A ZYGOTE
> AGAIN BEFORE YOUR EYES.

My counselor continued to explain that fathers, while useful in other ways (insemination, presumably), had no business feeding babies. Fathers were "not made" to do it. As for me, I was, and had to.

Of course, I wriggled and complained.

The counselor was patient, listening to my problems. And then she continued again, suggesting that if I just relaxed, let go, and got into it (perhaps a drop of Harvey's and a pink light bulb?), I'd enter a world so lovely, dark, and deep that I'd never want to leave. LLL sees nothing wrong with breast-feeding for years, as I've said. So much for promises to keep, and miles to go before you sleep. I would have been happy with a mere three months, some weight gain, and no tears.

As a final tip, my phone pal advised me to take off both my and my daughter's clothes while "doing it," forgetting (or ignoring) the well-known laxative effect of breast milk on infantile intestines.

Okay, it is a nice league of women, and they do have some good intentions, I'm sure. And the calls, and the help, are free. And they beckon you to an interesting place. A secret underworld of milky caverns, liquid walls, the thrumming of maternal blood, and the infinite filling of breasts.

Still, I stopped, and the daylight felt good.

Can I tell you a subversive secret? Once you stop counting your breast milk in drops, bottle-feeding is a huge pleasure. Mothers are re-lieved in more ways than one; fathers (and grandmothers), included; ba-bies, deeply sated. Moreover, articles have come out, for what they're worth (as you know, usually nothing) saying that breast-feeding might leech the calcium out of your bones, making you a future cripple. True to the doomsaying tone of articles such as these, you may suffer substan-tial (10 percent) bone loss even if you supplement your diet with as much as 2,100 milligrams daily. (And beware of kidney stones.)

Under the "every maternal action has an equal and opposite jour-nalistic reaction" principle," these articles must be counterbalanced by those that say bottle-feeding mothers are doomed to breast cancer. (Thrown into the same harsh purgatory reserved for first-time mothers over thirty, or—shriek!—women who have never borne children.)

You can't win unless you choose what's best for you and yours. Emma and I—and an increasing number of women—chose the bottle. Thank God it was still legal.

Why ever did I try the breast again? It wasn't that I wanted to prove Minerva wrong about my Mansfields, or that the League had got under my skin. I just felt like it, I don't know why. And luckily, this second child felt like it, too.

Yes: This child seemed privy to the breast-feeding cult. And what I learned, through our relative success, is that you really must keep faith with this process. No sitting through the U.S. Open. No late-night dinner parties chez your childless friends, at least not at first. Ultimately, what did us in was my attending preschool with Emma, during the so-called "separation" period. My being elsewhere than with Gabriel for a few hours each morning (usually my most copious time) seemed to hurt the process. And as he received more bottles, he nursed less, and then he took more bottles, and—well, La Leche isn't *all* wrong.

When he weaned himself, it was a bittersweet moment. A foreshadowing, perhaps, and a metaphor, for all future weanings, physical and emotional. Breast-feeding, I realized, was *power,* power of the most potent kind. No one else could do it but me, the mother, the only. When Gabriel cried, he cried for me, and when anyone else picked him up, be it my husband, mother, or—most challenging to my sense of specialness—baby-sitter, they brought him straight to *my* arms. He'd lie there, looking up, and I gave him all I could; I took him from anxiety to peace. Milk's a potent thing, a human manna.

From time to time I wished for it back, wished for him back on my once-magical breast. And I wondered, as I suppose all mothers do—is this the last time with the last child?

POSTSCRIPT: Just after I had weaned this second child of mine, putting him on powdered formula, new "wisdom" emerged attacking powdered formulas as being deficient in some vital nutrient.

One is torn between hating the papers for bringing bad news (and vowing not to read same), and being glad, deeply glad, that you've seen the story and can now do something about it—i.e., change formulas, go to liquid formulas, vary your formulas, etc. What you cannot do, however, is go back to the breast (La Leche may quibble on this, but trying to start up again involves mutual anguish on the part of mother and child). Hence the spiritual weariness of the conscientious mother: You're always finding out just one more vital tidbit.

My doctor said this particular tidbit was hocus-pocus, mumbo jumbo, nonsense. Forget it. Formulas are fine, have been for years. We all grew up on them. But (maddeningly) he advised me to alternate various formulas just to be safe. After exhuming and defrosting every last drop of my stored breast milk (how I wish I'd stored more), I found this unreassuring letter, by breast-feeding advocate Marvin S. Eiger, M.D., in the paper:

"[There are] some frighteningly incontrovertible facts about the infant formula industry, which has been guilty of numerous unfortunate errors of omission and commission. Unlike pharmaceuticals, infant formulas are unregulated by the F.D.A. Thus, as many have pointed out, the formula companies are involved in the largest uncontrolled experiment in human history. Human milk is still the nutritionally, immunologically and emotionally superior product. Make no mistake about it, because nature doesn't!"

Until the next article, maybe, which cites the pollutants in human breast milk. I'm waiting to see it. I'm sure it won't be long. And then, of course, the refutation, and the new poison-paranoia.

NINE

WHEREIN MOM AND DAD GO THE NURSE ROUTE AGAIN

As I said, we chose our second baby nurse because of her experience with breast-feeding mothers. Nicole knew it all: Drink lots and lots of water, she said. Get lots of rest. Sleep all night; don't get up to feed the baby.

I liked that bit about sleeping all night.

And you won't have to feed him more than once every four hours, either, she said.

Though it seemed that even *I* ate more often than that, I liked that, too.

I wondered if Nicole was perhaps a witch, but I didn't care at first, because I did indeed sleep through the night, and my son did, indeed, feed every four hours, and he gained weight, and we were all very happy.

Nicole was not only experienced, she ran an agency that specialized in multiple births. (She made us swear not to tell anyone she had taken the idiot's job with our singleton.) She assured us that if four-pound twins and three-pound triplets could be breast-fed (and they could; she had the remarkable photos to prove it), and if they could be kept on schedule—leading to that wonderful time when they slept through the night—so could our strapping baby boy.

Fantastic. Worth the fortune we were spending on her.

But she did have her faults. (The more you pay someone, the more significant the fault-finding.)

For one thing, the nails on this nurse were long red press-ons. They did not match her starchy whites because, unlike Minerva, Nicole wore either neon-colored tie-dyes that mesmerized my newborn, or T-shirts that advertised her nursing agency. Her clothing did not bother me, particularly; it seemed possible that she thought uniforms unnecessary, affected, or even demeaning. The scarlet claws did. They hinted at cruelty, seeming ideal for bringing deep gouges and resultant infection to the skin and the eyes of my newborn.

But this schedule business hooked me, nails or no nails. With a second child, the need to be superficially in control increases twofold: First, you feel you will go nuts with the two children both behaving unpredictably, and second, the fact you go nuts makes you furious, so you want action, order, *Achtung*.

You want to know, for instance, if you can take a shower or a nap at *any* point on a given day. Or cannot. Nicole not only guaranteed the shower and the nap, she promised that the baby would be sleeping through the night by the time she left. That meant within three weeks. (We decided to splurge this time: an extra week of meek dependency for an extra week of sleep.)

This night-sleep business sounded so miraculous that I overlooked not only the nails but Nicole's malevolent pale eyes, eyes that in my postpartum state recalled the Devil as portrayed in horror movies. They seemed to form concentric green pinwheels when she told me that some nurses, not those she would know or employ but had only *heard* about, had put drugs into their babies' bottles to make them sleep.

Thank you for sharing, Nicole.

I overlooked, too, the fact that Nicole snapped at me from time to time when I did something wrong, like change the channel from *Star Search* to something other than *Star Search*. She seemed the type who would not suffer fools gladly, and all new parents are foolish, no? I was, and still am. New, that is.

There were moments when Nicole, too, did "something wrong." I, Reader, was there on the scene with my caviling, carping, critical new mother's eye.

Cavil: She splashed water on my son's unhealed umbilicus, causing it to ooze. Then she tried to pull the oozy stump off.

Carp: When Gabriel developed a touch of infantile acne, she tried to fix it by smearing pore-sealing lanolin on the spots.

Crit: She bathed him, once, in cool water, under a ceiling fan that was whirring on High. And when I told her the water was too cold, she gave me the coldest stare, for I had not suffered her own folly.

But of course, of course, of course, anything was better than her leaving. Maxim One of getting help is that you weaken and lose your judgment. Like a woman married to the wrong man, like a child neglected by the wrong parent, like a diner in a lousy Borscht Belt restaurant, I wanted more of what I hated. I didn't want to be thrown out into the cold cruel.

In the way that ontogeny recapitulated phylogeny, the stages of parenthood, I believe, recapitulate the stages of childhood. I was still a toddler, working on separation (and its psychic twin, rebellion).

Nicole abandoned us for a set of twins (their parents pay better). She had been with us eight testy days, instead of several well-rested weeks. She was probably doing us a favor. At any rate, during our last hour together (in which she touched up her gluey manicure), she told us we'd be fine.

"But the baby's not sleeping through the night!" we accused.

"Oh, soon, he will, soon."

Soon. Thanks to blessed-cursed Nicole, I had been sleeping through the night, and still felt unkeeled. What would we do now?

We didn't trust her, but we didn't want her to be anyone else's nurse, either. We were jealous of those parents of twins. At least they had a nurse. What would we do?

Fingers flapping, Nicole offered to book us a new nurse through her own agency. No, we said, suspiciously.

Before she left, we hooked up to another nurse. Whispering, we interviewed her in our bedroom. We all sat on the bed, cozily, crabbing about Nicole. Subliminally, we searched for clues. We were developing some sort of expertise here. This one had nicely trimmed nails. She seemed friendly. She believed in the value of breast-feeding. On the other hand, if you didn't breast-feed, that was okay, too. She looked at our son and called him "Too-toose!" That was cute. Her own name was Dena. Call me Deeny, she said. That, too, fell on the pro-cuteness side of the ledger.

We had found this Deeny through a large agency. She whispered that Nicole was *terrible* to leave us in the lurch, that her agency *never* let people do that. Deeny said, You're supposed to stay on the job you're on, no matter what. After all, people really need you, or they wouldn't be going to all the trouble and expense.

Go, Deeny, go. Take me, my husband, and my baby. Nurse us, Deeny!

"I'll help you out," she agreed.

Magic words, again.

And she did help. She was the kindest by far of the three, and kindness is one of those things that can't be bought. (Except in this case.)

She would say to me, when I was on the verge of helpless blubbering, "Don't cry, Soney, you'll give yourself the postpartum!"

That made me laugh as well as blubber.

Then she'd check to see if I really had stopped crying, and if I hadn't, she'd make me some really strong tea.

But did you think she had no oddities?

She did. For one thing, her word for baby's solid waste was not the professional "BM" but rather *"doo-dee,"* pronounced deliberately, slowly, with a good long pause in the middle. I suppose that went with the name "Too-toose."

And here is Deeny's list of what nursing women should not eat: lettuce, celery, cucumbers, peppers, oranges, tomato sauce, beans, peanuts. . . . An exhaustive list, actually, and most of it quite vital to human survival. Any time the baby cried, she'd say, "Did you eat something?" Well, of course I had. A lettuce leaf, maybe even with a slice of tomato. And a cucumber. Splashed with oil and vinegar. I did it, and I was proud!

"Well, now," she'd say, "you see what's happening to the child? Baby gonna make a soft, soft *dooo-deeee* on account of that."

Deeny also loved condensed milk, three days old, straight from the can. That, and red snapper. Snapper day and night and night and day. A harmless pair of vices, really, and I wouldn't mention them but for the fact that I had to keep shopping to keep her in Borden-snapper heaven.

I remember that on her first day of work, she asked me, "What's for dinner?" I excused myself for a little cry. I—who associate cooking with aprons, heat, and boredom—who have yet to come to terms with the secret link between "mother" and "stove"—thought she would take care of this pots-and-pans business. Or at least do what we did—order in, open a yogurt, heat up a can of soup, have a sandwich. She found all that a bit bohemian, decadent. Which of course is the point of our lives, or had been.

"What's for dinner?" I can still work up some tears over that demand. We thought we were paying *you*, Deeny!

Also unpleasant is the tendency of nurses to type your child. If Minerva had tuned us in to Emma's "little temper," labeling her (despite our open minds), Deeny let us know that our little son was "scared of everything." This was because he tended to leap whenever Emma screeched. She has since stopped screeching, and he has stopped leaping and is—at the moment—scared only of men with matted beards.

Eventually, we realized we didn't need Deeny, not desperately. (And desperate was how we'd been up to now.) She suddenly seemed slightly in the way, and we weren't such amateurs anymore. We felt hemmed in. We wanted to play by ourselves, make our own huge errors, call in for our own Chinese food.

It hurt to say good-bye. Deeny's maternality had touched me. When she left, I really cried. Such is the power of the parental separation trauma. I wondered if it was worth it to let someone help you if they're going to leave in the end, anyway. If you're going to have to face things yourself, small and wretched as you sometimes feel.

Deeny said, "I *told* you not to cry," and I cried harder.

Saying she would call me later in the day, she hugged me.

I wobbled back into my own life. I forgot that she said she'd call me, and so did she.

I still had a baby-sitter, though.

TEN

QUEENIE IN THE HOME

When Minerva, my first baby nurse, left, my husband returned to work. I found myself swamped with writing assignments. As I'd envisioned myself as someone not "stopped" by childbearing, I had made irresponsible boasts to various people in the publishing industry. I had told the guys at *The New York Times,* for instance, for whom I was writing free-lance Arts pieces, to treat me the way they did before. Amazingly, they took me at my word and gave me work.

I called Minerva and asked her if she knew anyone who'd make a good part-time sitter for a newborn.

After the briefest pause, she said she did.

She told us of her cousin by marriage, "a bit stout," who could keep house (i.e., mind the baby, vacuum the rug) for us.

The name of this prospective sitter was Queenie April.

Queenie was not a bit stout, she was huge: tall, fat, round, totemic. She came from the Caribbean. Her skin was black; her teeth were white. She wore bright, tight clothing (a far cry from Minerva's starched tailoring) and shouted, "HOW YOU *DOIN'!!*" when she strolled through the door. She also favored small little hats with stiff, netted poufs.

The baby disappeared into Queenie's arms, which easily outdid the girth of my postpartum thighs, which says something.

I relaxed with Queenie. I liked her.

Someone once told me that there was something atavistic about all these black women taking care of all these white babies. What she meant was, as you walked into the parks on any given afternoon, what you saw was a recreation of the antebellum South. Some who saw Queenie ended up saying that she reminded them of *Gone With the Wind,* or of certain kitschy salt-and-pepper shakers—then wondered if saying that was racist. I suppose it was.

Talking to her relatives on the phone, Queenie called me her "mistress," a locution I found bizarre. She hummed spirituals; she praised the Lord; she tittered when I gave her a compliment—"Oh, no, you make me laugh!" There was a stylized jollity about her, but at the same time she was genuinely happy and made others so.

Queenie had been working with children since the age of fourteen. The oldest of ten children whom she had helped raise, she had been sent abroad, after the death of her father, and told to make money and send most of it home. Her first job, she told me, was for a South American she called "the Governor." She could not get more specific about her boss, but it seemed he was not married but had a daughter, and Queenie was to be her nanny.

When I met her, Queenie was thirty-four. The girl was grown, and Queenie sometimes wondered aloud what had become of her. She only knew the little child, of course, not the adult. Nevertheless, Queenie talked about her in the present tense. "Oh, Eva would like this toy. She likes dolls." Or, "This is Eva's favorite color"—shocking pink. Realizing that she was dwelling on things impossible—that is, the current life of a rich white girl—Queenie would grow more and more wistful. Abruptly, she'd change the subject to my child, Emma, right there (for the moment) in front of her.

"I think she gonna be real smart, that Emma. A doctor!"

Queenie, who had her share of medical problems, did not like to be sad. In fact, she seemed to refuse to be, and said of a sad thing: "I won't let it spoil my joy." And then she'd start singing again.

It's a crazy thing, hiring a person to love your child. You hope the child loves the baby-sitter, but not too much. You want both to know you're the mother, the one who will love the child forever, no matter what. You know that that other relationship, the one that strangely resembles love, is going to end. How and when? You don't know. Will it hurt your baby-sitter? Will it not hurt her? Will she come back to visit? Will she not? Will she fly the coop, abruptly, without warning? Will she do something so bad that you'll have to let her go? And what will you say to your child about any of it?

Some of the experienced sitters know all these dynamics. They've loved before, and they've left—that's why they're now in your house. So, instead of attending your child's school play, they race to get home. They'd rather get back to their own hours, their own families, their own lives. Sure, they love you all, but when the bell rings, they're out of there.

So who are these people to us? Family? Employees? "Retainers"? This may be the most complex issue of motherhood, and like most issues of modern motherhood, money hovers somewhere near the center.

We pay people to care for our babies.

From this one hub spins a wheel of many spokes. Because we pay them, we may fire them, at any time, and they know it. Because we pay them a certain amount, they may leave us one day for someone who pays them more. Because we pay them, we resent them slightly for not being what they are supposed to be: everything to our kids, but not too much; clever enough to handle any emergency and the reading of complex tales, but not so clever that they get a better—or a better-paying—job.

Doubting their cleverness and their loyalty, we enroll our kids in programs, so that at least we are "sure" they're getting the most out of their day. That leads to a complex of other paid parental surrogates: the tumbling instructor, the preschool teacher, the music-dance-storytime leader. Parents I know say things like: "At least I know my kid's not at home all day with the soaps on," or, "At least she's with someone who can get down on the floor with her," or, "At least he's with someone who can speak English."

Does that mean that we're not entirely confident about the primary employee? Of course it does. Horror stories abound that feature everything from nannies who take their charges to McDonald's every day (where they meet their friends, the other nannies, and everyone eats fries), to those who never take the child out at all. I have even heard of a sitter who left the home during a toddler's lengthy naptime, picking up a few extra dollars upstairs at another job. That last sitter was exposed by a neighbor, after several months had passed.

Every time I go to the park with my kids, I see something I don't like, nannywise. So does every other mother. And we all think, well, *my* baby-sitter would never do that. She loves the child, she is so happy. And we pay her pretty well, don't we?

Surprisingly, much inter-parent chatter seems to center on how *little* the child's caretaker is paid. "You're paying *what*? And she doesn't clean? We pay *half* that, and she sits for us every night!" This kind of talk is especially characteristic—or perhaps simply most flagrantly so—of those who can afford to pay well.

A recent playground conversation:

My husband and I bump into a thirtyish couple with their two sons. My husband knows the father from the office. The man makes a real bundle, still, on Wall Street. His wife, a former musician, does not work outside the home. They have a live-in housekeeper who takes care of the boys, aged six and eight. They have had several, all of whom left abruptly, and they don't seem to know why. They aren't troubled by it, though.

To me, due to my instincts and perhaps borne out by some studies somewhere, continuity of care ranks close to quality of care, but then again, my kids are younger, and then again, I've had two sitters in three years (Queenie is gone), so who am I to talk?

This couple is not troubled by the discontinuity, because, they confide, the new woman they have living in their house is incredibly "cheap." Meaning, they pay her more cheaply than they have paid anyone before.

What are her hours? I ask, wondering what it must be like to have a live-in, so that you can go out at night without always calling someone. Apart from the expense, it must be nice for the kids to have the same person at home at night that they have during the day (providing they like her).

Oddly, the question of whether or not the *child* likes the baby-sitter does not come up for all parents. Most mothers I ask swear that *they love* their employee—demonstrating that tendency to think that the one you've hired is faultless, until the day you fire her in shock. They assume their kids feel exactly the same way. Other mothers, myself among them, gravitate first toward sitters who are loved by their children—regardless of their adult people skills. Each technique has its mortal consequences.

Sure, they say, they like the sitter, she's great, and the kids "seem to" like her, though it's hard to tell (you could ask them), but soon the conversation turns back to the hours.

The new sitter's hours turn out to be quite rough.

"She's on day and night," they brag.

No lunch? No supper? Break, I meant. Ostensibly, they feed her. She'll work better if they feed her.

"No," both parents chimed in. "Once you start giving time off, they come to expect it. Oh, sure, she can grab a sandwich," says the wife. "But suppose I gave her lunch off. And then one day *I* didn't want to be home at lunchtime. Then where would I be?"

"Or suppose we let her have an hour off on a Friday afternoon," adds the husband. "That could turn out to be a Friday that we needed her to pack up for our country house."

Why, I asked, would anyone accept these terms?

"Because they have to," said the wife, conspiratorially. "They're desperate."

Maybe that's why you and I see so much sullenness, so much hostility in the park, among the sitters. Why we see kids crying while the sitters go on chatting to their friends. We see kids being smacked, or ignored to the point of quasi-abandonment, or a sitter simply tutting and grumbling to no one in particular, "Kid drivin' me crazy." It's not that all mothers are perfect. But there seems to be something extra going on here. Money and its cousins, class and clout.

Sitters, particularly those without agency or specialization, are somewhat powerless in the money department. They are competing in a crowded market. Many have no papers; some are outrageously poor; few are capable of taking off into a new, more lucrative career. If class is determined by lifestyle in this country, they are certainly on the bottom rung. They seem relatively cloutless, too.

But they *aren't* without clout.

They have clout with the children, where it counts. In the gut. Their desperation is something to fear; despair makes people act strangely. If they are at their wits' end in terms of survival, they owe us, and our children, nothing.

Love cannot, in any case, be bought. It must be earned. On both sides.

The next time someone who lives in a huge house brags to me

about how little she pays, or chides me for being too generous (double her sitter's salary and that's still too little), I'm going to ask her, How much are your kids worth?

Or, more to the point: How much are you worth? That's who's getting replaced: Mother. How much for a reasonable facsimile, for a good-faith effort?

And there is no good answer.

I chose my second sitter, Mia, because she seemed earnest, responsible, and motherly. There was a way that she touched my daughter's head, on the day they met, gently tucking a wisp of hair back under her hat. And Emma, at one and a half, could show me, if not tell me, that she liked her.

Did *I* like her? As far as she and I were concerned, there could be no worse match. She is shy, I am a chatterbox. She is conservative to the point of not wanting to have a television set in her home, or ever seeing a movie. I love TV, and my library—not to mention my brain—features erotic art and literature. She is frugal and practical. I am flighty and impulsive (I can afford to be).

In the beginning, I scare her. When I walk through the door, she jumps, literally, in the air. And she does things that worry me. Why, for instance, did she spend the first few months of Emma's naptime gently scraping some imaginary dirt off the walls with what sounded like a little brush? What was that brush? A toothbrush? *My* toothbrush?

I thought, at the time, that she was eccentric (no rarity in the world of sitters), or that she was an incredibly meticulous housekeeper, but she is neither. She was nervously looking for something to do. She never sits down with a copy of the *National Enquirer* (actually, she reads the *Times*), even when the house is clean and quiet, and for that I suppose I am grateful.

When the children are sick, she is at her best. Mopping the brow, reheating the broth, she is more mother than I could ever be. When Emma had a severe diaper rash, she stood her up in the kitchen sink and washed her bottom with warm, soapy water, and not once but many times. Then she let Emma run around without a diaper, so that she wouldn't chafe, wiping up accidents from the carpet without complaint.

She loves my rambunctious girl with patience and even wit and mischief. The smile she rarely shows me is big and wide. And she loves my sweet-souled boy with a physical fervor I would not thought her capable of, kissing him on the neck with a loud *mmm-mmmfff!*

Apart from an interesting character study, she is a study in that fine, fine line between employee and blood relative. Is she with us, or is she not? When the clock strikes six, she is out the door, and nothing—not even the offer of overtime cash—will keep her away from her own, very private, life.

This reminds me that fond Mia may one day hurt my children by parting from them. The clock will strike for the last time, and she will permanently go. Perhaps she will work for other people, kiss *their* babies' necks with a loud *mmm-mmmmf!* This is as sad as the prospect of divorce: How can it be? Didn't we feel what we thought we felt?

I comfort myself with the fact that she does, still, visit her former work family, but it is small comfort when I see how closely she and my children are bonded. Gabriel, in particular, has known her since birth.

Does he know that I am his real and only mother?

Perhaps I should have paid better attention to the bonding business. I did carry him, I did nurse him, I do love him with a blinding passion that would make dying for him a snap, and I think I delivered him a fine daddy and a good, patient sitter. I think I, too, am becoming a good, patient sitter, a better mother for him now than I was for his sister, back then in the Year One.

But did I do *everything* for my children, at all times, always? You never can. There were things I did for Emma, crazy, time-consuming things like infant massage, that I simply could not stand to do again. At least not with a paid instructor.

That leads us into the next chapter.

ELEVEN

WHEREIN BABY SIMPLY MUST HAVE A MASSAGE

My poor, deprived child, I mused, as I flicked by a blurb about baby massage in a recent magazine (it was couched between ads for *Money* magazine and Armani eyewear). Nearly nine months old, Emma had never been massaged by a certified therapist (or, for that matter, spent a day of beauty at Elizabeth Arden). Thank goodness I noticed in time, or nearly so: The optimal age for this treatment is, I soon learned, somewhere before six months. Is six months too old? Yes, probably, I was told. At that age, many try to crawl away from the ministering hands. But if it's so nice, why would they try to—never mind. I called up a baby masseuse and decided to see for myself.

The woman I called had long taught mothers to massage their babies at a well-known parenting center in New York. She has trained other masseuses to teach mothers and other masseuses. If the world of infant massage were an endless, sensual spiral, this woman would be at the pulsing center of it.

For fifty dollars, the masseuse (I'll call her Kiki) agreed to make a home visit for both my ancient (in massage terms) daughter and my friend Pat's premature eight-week-old son. Premature infants, the massage lore (and some scientific study) goes, are ideal candidates. "The neuro-chemical effect of skin-to-skin contact" is credited with improving their circulation, growth, and digestion. "It's also a beautiful, intense exchange," said Kiki.

Here is the principle of the thing, as outlined in one of several massage books: "Each stroke helps to soothe out mental and physical tensions that accompany the stresses of babyhood." I wonder if *you* realized how very stressful, how mentally and physically tense, babyhood was. I had not, and I'm glad they told me. I had thought my baby was happy.

Babies, continues this book, become "aware" of their bodies through massage. They "relax with pleasure." You, the parent, "get in touch with positive feelings. . . ." You need to, especially after being informed that your baby, pre-massage, had not been happy. Finally, through closeness, warmth, and eye contact, you and your baby enter the crucial bonding process.

Here I must break away and complain that incessant hints about bonding (and corollary, unspoken threats about failure to bond) always seem to precede the expenditure of money on professional expertise. As one pediatrician, wisely choosing to remain anonymous, says, "Why is it that upper-class intellectuals always need to be told how to love their kids?"

Because there's always someone telling us?

Anyway, if you, too, are nagged by the *B*-word, there can be no harm in proceeding. Proceed with a naked baby who has not just eaten. (In any case, you may prefer a diapered baby; massage relaxes bladder and bowel along with everything else.) Be sure the room is warm. Use a vegetable oil, not baby oil, which contains petroleum. (TNT.) Light touch. Here goes.

Start on the front. Scalp: very gently, in tiny circles. Pretend you're an apprentice washer at Vidal Sassoon, with a fairly small, bald client. Face: Smooth from center out to sides (disregard puzzled stare). Do earlobes. Chest: up to the shoulders and down to the arms. Then across the chest diagonally across the middle, then the opposite diagonal. (I've heard this process described differently, so who knows?) Arms: from shoulder to wrist in one long stroke (Indian style—away from the heart). Then from wrist to shoulder (Swedish style, toward the heart). Encircle upper arm and squeeze, then go down the length of the arm, doing little squeezes. Then back up again. Open the hands and massage the palms. Play with the fingers (why not?). Abdomen: clockwise circles. Now, the fancy maneuver: With outside edge of hands, press down from abdomen to tops of legs. "This directly pushes gas out." A bonding bonus!

Legs: Hold ankle, encircle leg with other hand, then stroke down from thigh to ankle (Indian). Then back up again (Swedish). Massage thighs and calves in little squeezes, going up and down. With your thumb and index finger, massage ankles in tiny circles, play with toes (why not?), massage the soles. Try to remember what, if anything, you know about reflexology.

Lora Dudley, mother of Amy and devotee of Kiki, told me that when Kiki had visited her and her two friends (for the combined price of seventy-five dollars), "it was really great. She brings the oil and the soft music; you bring the naked baby. One kid peed; Kiki was so accepting."

Another mother, who had traveled from Princeton to meet Kiki, had heard that after a massage, even colicky babies have slept for five hours. So, did *her* baby sleep for five hours? "I don't know, but during the session, she sure got quiet for a little while." How was she on that ride in from Princeton?

"New mothers can feel scared of their own babies," says Dudley. "But Kiki tells you, Don't squeeze the knee. But she doesn't say it like, Oh, you dumb idiot. And she says it before you get there, so you don't think, Oy, I already touched it.

"You never feel, my baby is failing massage. In fact, it was the first time I didn't *think* we'd flunked something, you know, like Lamaze or breast-feeding or Gymboree."

I am sad to report that within ten minutes of our own private session with Kiki, Pat and I did flunk. Our experiment came to a standstill. Emma, who had been rather big about the squeezing of her thighs and the palpation of her toes, abruptly decided to blow the joint and get scooting on the floor. Aaron, who preferred the swaddled state to the nude, was nonetheless game at first, looking intently at his mother as she stroked his soles. But when the action moved to his tiny, pulsing middle, Aaron shuddered, spat up, and finally resorted to wild arm-flailing, which is "Bonding is now over!" in any language.

Kiki continued her lesson on a teddy bear (*he* cooperated), and I'm sure many babies and more new mothers would have been amused by her attentions. More frequently, like most baby masseuses, she ministers to classes. There, the "beautiful, intense exchange" is guaranteed among like-minded, no-developmental-stone-unturned parents. What is guaranteed for the babies? Not terribly much.

TWELVE

WHEREIN BABY NEEDS A WORKOUT TAPE

Flicking through *American Baby*, a "free" publication for mothers, I see a blurb endorsing a tape called *Baby's First Workout:* "From the title, you might wonder how an infant can possibly exercise when she can't even stand."

Note the understanding of the absurdity of "exercise" for infants, not to mention exercise videos. Note the nonsexist use of the pronoun "she." These people have thought their argument through. We're on your side, they're saying. We're hip. But do buy the tape anyway, because:

"That's not the message here. This video covers . . . the simple motor skills children are normally able to accomplish during their first year—"

Stop right there! Did you say "normally able to accomplish"? Then why do we need to send away for help?

They're just getting to that.

"—and showing ways you can monitor those skills."

Oh, the normal accomplishments (i.e., looking, playing, moving) of infancy need to be "monitored"? Book that shrink for the year 2020! And on to this year's expert, instructor Patti Gerard Hannan, a "former gymnast, NASA researcher and preschool teacher—"

Not to mention Rhodes scholar, trainer of full-bred Weimaraners, and toque-wearing Cordon Bleu. Of course I'm kidding. Still, the founder of "the Gerard Method" *is* possessed of a giddy set of all-American attributes—a perfect role model for any "she." Hannan, we learn, has developed a way of "monitoring" your child—

"through creative play exercise. No, she doesn't encourage jumping jacks and push-ups—"

And a good thing, too, for it's the rare three-monther who can manage them with good form.

". . . just simple things like having your child visually follow an object from side to side."

Or else!

Seeing no alternative, I ordered the tape. By the way, at thirty bucks, it's truly expensive, but no child should be forced into a life of bench-warming simply because his parents are too darned cheap. And it does come with a wonderful chart for "measuring your child's skill development." Not only can you measure this development (which should hurtle along—if you buy the tape), but you can measure it *against* average development—proof positive that you are gaining that competitive edge.

Once purchased, the tape informs me of the athlete's philosophy, which stresses the "deeper implications" of the most basic skills (head-turning, crawling, pulling up to stand). All these, she says, influence "your child's development."

Hannan reiterates her credits as gymnast, student of weightlessness at NASA, professional coach, and mother of an eight-year-old girl (portrayed in baton-twirling outfit, holding a large flag). We are led to understand that this girl is the product of a mother who, quite properly, took her early motor development as no laughing matter.

Hannan tells the camera that she was terribly "concerned" that her daughter be provided with "a good foundation in motor skills." Straight after giving birth, she says, she sought out ways of judging the child's physical abilities. She vigilantly looked for "key periods" to "promote skill mastery." To her dismay, she found that "no scientific, systematic system of skill building existed."

Those were the days.

Then Hannan decided to get into the action.

Heads up, newborns! (Can't get them up? Try harder.)

Hannan takes us on a visual tour through a playground. She highlights the subtle, yet ominous, implications of the monkey-bar scene.

"It doesn't take long," she says somberly, "to notice how different [children] are at play." From her own expert observation that some children are better at running, others at climbing, some superior in strength, and others in agility, she concludes: "*These differences are no accident.* They're based on heredity, physical maturity, body size, and neuromuscular development." When to start worrying? "Right away," says Hannan. So thank goodness you have bought the tape, are watching it, and worrying yourself sick.

(By the way, has Hannan ever compared the activity level of parents and children who sit broodily watching exercise tapes with those who actually get out and randomly, happily play?)

Here is some more scientific information: "Specialists have long known that youngsters develop motor skills at varying rates but in the same sequence," and that "learning takes place most readily during certain growth periods." So what? This is like saying that there is a time to crawl, a time to walk, the former generally preceding the latter. Enter the concept of failure: "Failure to master these skills in a step-by-step progression . . . will affect all subsequent skill development." You mean a normal child can fail to get around? Will he then fail to climb? To run? To jump rope? Hannan isn't saying no: When learning is "delayed beyond the critical stage, the skill is more difficult, or even impossible, to learn well." Regrettably, she says, some children are not coached, but "left on their own." These poor souls "do not always master the full range of skills needed for thorough development." So that's how couch potatoes are made.

We know that the skills that Hannan is talking about are not those of the climbing frame, the pep squad, or the Olympic team. After all, the "skills" covered in this interminable tape, *those of an infant from one to twelve months,* will be mastered by all healthy individuals—unless they are chained to a wall from dawn to dusk. No child has to be taught to turn his face, to lift his head, or to stand. Hannan's implication of lifelong disqualification from sport, or NASA, seems a bit farfetched.

Covering that base, she periodically adds: Have *fun*.

Covering another, she also advises avid parents (her market) to be careful when "playing and exercising your baby." In fact, she tells you to consult your pediatrician before beginning this program. This may be a good way to see if your pediatrician is an idiot or not. If he tells you you need to go on the program, he is.

If, God forbid, your child lags behind the charted average (did you dawdle and not order the tape until baby was three months old?), you are again advised to consult your child's doctor "immediately." That way, the deficit may be caught, and corrected, in time for the next charted activity. Here, too, is a chance to see if your doctor is a hysterical alarmist or the saner type—who will tell you to keep your baby but throw away your chart.

After these medical provisos, the refrain returns: "This is a system of creative play. So have *fun.*" As for the baby, "let he or she [sic] know that this is a *fun* time." There are only so many ways to say "fun" on one thirty-dollar tape, so on with the details.

To the extent I could watch this tape (limited), I learned that for the 0–3-month-old child, good exercise involves getting tickled by a feather, watching balls move from side to side, turning (or trying to turn) the head when persistently summoned by a jangling toy or the sound of Patti Gerard Hannan mispronouncing your name, and other such "bonding" activities that, in life, are often are accomplished without the accompaniment of taped narration.

I raced ahead to the end of the tape, where I found babies being taught to "Pat-a-Cake" ("we lined up some champion patty-cakers," she chirps), crawl (reluctantly) up and down an ironing board in pursuit of an elusive ball, and do the aptly named "puppet walk." Aptly named, for you the parent are making the child walk "properly," as walking is "the basis of all further gross motor development." So pull those strings nice and taut, folks.

I exaggerate to prove my point. But that is quid pro quo: So does this humorless tape.

THIRTEEN

WHEREIN BABY NEEDS A WORKOUT CLASS

ometimes a humorless tape is not enough. You will be receiving invitations to exercise your child in public, where there is greater likelihood of having fun. If you are the parent of a child older than six months, you have probably been to Gymboree or one of its rivals.

"It's like a cult," says one mother, half-admiringly. "We have to go. Everybody goes, and nobody knows why they do." Over the past two years, enrollment has skyrocketed, a tribute to marketing and parental paranoia.

For city parents, trapped in claustrophobia with a squirming baby and tiny flat, Gymboree represents a Way Out. This is the beginning of the let-somebody-help-you treadmill, and it is addictive. So, more and more parents find themselves blearily sleepwalking toward those padded, primary-colored rooms where children romp and parents ease their solitude.

"It's where you meet everyone in your neighborhood, at least the ones with kids," says one East Side New Yorker. On rainy days, when you can't go to the park, it's there. On frosty days, when you'd rather die than go to the park, it's there. "What're we going to do at home when the weather stinks?" says a mother of a thirteen-month old boy. "Play patty-cake till we drop?"

Clearly, not.

For working mothers, there is another, sharp angle. It's guilt, the old familiar: If you're not home with your child, how on earth do you know what's going on in there? How do you know he's not propped in front of *The Young and the Restless,* sucking a dirty forefinger? How, to be more positive, are you going to make sure that he has a happy, fulfilling time (life)? Gymboree plays that angle, offering not merely a release for mad housewives but also "Play with a Purpose." You know what that means. An edge for your kids. A shot at the brass ring. One fears raising a klutz in an era of aerobic superbabes. One fears missing out on the happening thing.

Gymboree brings structured movement to infants as young as three months of age. Like gaunt missionaries to blobby savages, it redefines the world in terms of virtue. Direction. Accomplishment. (If we really wanted those things, why would we have had children?)

"Play with a Purpose": Is this a spin-off of our own cellulitophobia? (Most mothers, postpartum, realize that not only have *they* been reproducing, but so has their cellulite.) Is it the trailing comet tail of eighties excess, where children must vie for the Olympics—or pen a short story about how they chose Harvard instead? Is it perhaps a boomer wish to step—now vicariously—into Romper Room? (It must be no accident that the very name of the place recalls the Mouseketeer chant to "Join the jamboree!") Perhaps it's just one more aspect of our harried nineties lives: Swallow the bait, account for your hours, and nagging guilt won't find you slacking off.

Gymboree, as I would shortly learn, works like this: You walk into a large, gym-mat-covered room filled with brightly colored objects that are meant to be slid on, rocked on, climbed, twirled around in, and bounced. You are greeted by a name-tagged teacher (we'll call her "Sherri") who smiles and sticks a name tag on your child. (This fake heartiness evokes visions of pyramid schemes and dental conventions.) The child—perhaps still unable to walk—is now led into a circle to hear the opening strains of the Gymboree anthem. It is sung to the tune of the Oscar Mayer song, or "My baloney has a first name." Parents and Sherri typically do all the singing. They have to.

Other organized activities involve "popcorn," which translates into pounding on an inflatable log, riding on the aforementioned log, catching bubbles, listening to jingling bells, and playing "soccer": Parents hold their babies, swatting their legs at the flying balls.

Gymboree might be harmless, and it does pass the time—forty-five minutes go by in a flash. What may be harmful is the insistence on developmental "edge," that Harvard-Olympus-bound nonsense. Classes are given in units called "semesters." At Open House (where parents, too, wear name tags), teachers earnestly point out that children will learn balance by going to Gymboree—or as they put it, class will "stimulate their vestibular coordination." There is talk of "developing upper-arm strength" and of "ocular tracking." One exercise involves pulling your baby's arms out away from his body and then—*Voila!*—crossing them in front of his chest like the arms of a straitjacket. First, right over left. Then, left over right. The sequence is sure to evoke "maximum right and left-brain activity." And you thought your child would walk and talk without signing up for the course!

Songs are sung with great bombast, as though they were hymns. While leading a jocular round of "The Noble Duke of York," Sherri suddenly stopped, insisting that parents and children sing and clap at the same time. *Why,* Sherri? (No one dared ask.) She told us: "So that both play and verbal advantages are being achieved." Then one little baby had jingle bells systematically rung into his left ear, and then his right. This demonstrated the fact that, at his age, babies supposedly do not hear in stereo. (Well, not if you put the bells on one side, then the other, they don't.)

Insubordination does not go over well. When I tried to take Emma up on the inflatable log, she was nearly suspended, because I mistakenly had her face me instead of another baby. "They have to look at each other and socialize," said our leader. And when the class was told to get into formation for a parade, Emma broke formation and started chasing balls. Wrong. Then she started climbing ramps. Not now, Emma. She also got on a trampoline that was set before a mirror. File in, kid.

This is one of those opportunities to see your child as others see him.

Smiling, Sherri kept picking up my anarchist and plopping her back into the formation. Good luck, Sherri, and keep taking that B-complex!

My friend who teaches at Bank Street, a major center for child study and teacher training in New York, thinks that structured environments like the one at Gymboree are the opposite of what childhood is about, distracting children from what interests them, dragging them over for some vestibular coordination. She says that ultimately, such pressure (accompanied or unaccompanied by a smile) could do some harm to a child's self-esteem.

Studies have shown no *physical* long-term benefits to exercise programs: no future reduction of obesity, no greater athletic prowess, no competitive edge. In fact, the American Academy of Pediatrics, in a policy statement, has said that not only has there "been no data to suggest that structured programs will advance skills or provide any long-term benefit to normal infants," but that "[t]he possibility exists that adults may exceed the infants' physical limitations by using structured exercise programs." That means anything from stretching a baby's leg beyond the point where he wants it to go to exhausting a toddler mentally and physically. The AAP recommends, therefore, that a parent provide a "minimally structured play environment." Sort of like what most of us have right at home. Minimal structure. A lawn. A sofa. A tree. Some steps.

Still, the way Emma used the place, she seemed to have one of the best times of her life over at maximally structured Gymboree. So did my husband. Apparently, a lot of fathers (who show up in numbers on weekends) get a real kick out of the equipment. There are lots of things to get lost in, and even I found it fun to see my child shrieking delightedly, out of the earshot of our sensitive neighbors.

When, more recently, I took my son to an open house at rival (and I think less phony) Playorena, he was delighted with every bit of it, the rolling on the log, the bouncing of the balls, the looking in the mirror. (Best of all, he liked the sight of other babies.) Indeed, many children complain (a euphemism for bawling) when they have to pack up and go.

Some parents, however, do not bawl when it's time to leave.

"It's like Ronald McDonald on speed," one mother whispered to me. A lifeless character called "Gymbo" was veering toward her child, who was unfortunately stuck in a multicolored chute. Gymbo, who has a crooked smile (and can, incidentally, be purchased through the glossy Gymboree catalog), was only trying to say "Bye-bye!" He—actually, it was Sherri—was waving his puppet arm up and down. It was a quarter past. The next pack of future athletes was being unloaded from their strollers.

These days, my kids and I head over to the park. The best things in life (fresh air, good humor, youth) are actually still free.

FOURTEEN

KEEPING BABY ALIVE: THE EVERYTHING CAN KILL HIM CHAPTER

S hould you and your child overexert yourselves, you will need to know a few lifesaving tips. Working from the fear angle, a good many people are now teaching lifesaving courses for new mothers. Lifesaving techniques are, in themselves, a wonderful idea. What makes some of the safety entrepreneurs notorious, however, is the pressure they put on mothers to take their courses and, once within the course, to feel blood terror over every possible life contingency.

BABY GOES TO SLEEP! *eeekk!!!* BABY EATS! *eeeeek!* BABY TAKES A BATH! *call 911!!!* BABY CRAWLS THROUGH AN UN-TIDY HOUSE!

OH-MY-GOD!!

I recently saw an ad for a newsletter that promised to warn parents, on a regular basis, of the many *seemingly* safe things they were doing that were, in actual fact, terribly dangerous! *Terribly!* Subscribe and save your baby's life!

For instance, said this ad, "You give your baby a bath. Afterward, you apply talcum powder to your baby. DANGEROUS MISTAKE." (In red letters.) Or: "Your baby has a rash on the buttocks. You apply Vaseline, then a disposable diaper. DANGEROUS MISTAKE." Subscribe now, and learn "The truth about plastic pacifiers. The truth about disposable diapers. The truth about vaporizers. The truth about fluoride. *And more.*"

Since I know just about all the truth I can stand, I decided to stick with a CPR refresher. My second child was about to be born, and I'd recently heard and read about an instructor I'll call Michael. The man is known. He has been on several morning shows. He has been written up in the papers. He has taught CPR to the stars. He has written a safety book, available at your bookstore. He is the Safety Man, strong arms, baby mannequins, and all. Tons of people, whose children are still safe and alive, swear by him.

After giving birth to my son, I found myself overwhelmed by fatigue, inertia, and churlishness. I couldn't decide if I really needed to be refreshed on CPR or not. My thoughts rambled. Maybe I'll send the baby-sitter. She's never taken CPR. Yeah. No: Maybe I'll go, if Paul goes, too. He can take notes; I can fall asleep on his shoulder. Yeah, I think that's what I'll do.

In the end, I sent my baby-sitter, Mia, who is, as I've mentioned before, mature and unhysterical.

She came back shaken.

"It is very scary," she said in her cryptic way. It was hard to coax more details out of her, but she implied that Michael had told the class several horrifying tales intended to jolt them from complacency into safety-consciousness. She, who had raised two children already (without the help of the course), seemed to be trying to calm herself down and resume a normal perspective on the world and its dangers.

When I finally hauled myself in for the course, I found I never did calm myself down. I emerged a changed and shaken mom. This happened two years ago, and I am still *on alert*. My toilet seat is down, and locked, the bathroom door is locked, my burners have guards on them, I cook only on the back burners and pursue small coins and paper clips and stray buttons as the instruments of annihilation they are. I am aware that even pricey perfume is a poison, and that children can and will do the darndest and deadliest things—when you least expect it. So I have come to expect anything.

I attribute this altered (burdened?) state to Michael, whose incredible effect on me and others is obviously intentional. Of course, he is on the side of the Good—safety is good, danger is bad. "He's there to scare you," say his defenders. "He gives you a hundred forty percent, so you're left with eighty percent, which is better than nothing," calculates Sue, who used to work on Wall Street. Donna, another Michael veteran, says he is a "brainwasher," but enjoyed being brainwashed—this way, she figures, she will be able to function on automatic during an actual emergency. Ellen bitterly describes the course as "fanatical," "horrendous." I am somewhere in between. The problem for me is that constant fight-or-flight is best known for causing mammals (including parents) to burn out, expire, conk out on the night watch.

Michael begins his three-and-a-half hour lecture thus:

"We're speaking about life and death. Any moment, you could be faced with the sight of a dead child."

We grow ashen as he proceeds to count the ways. You might be giving your child a bath. You need a dry towel. You turn your back. All of a sudden, the child's lips are blue. He's dying. Or: You could be having a barbecue in the backyard. You answer the phone. Your child heads for the pool. A variant: Maybe you're letting your older one watch the younger one inside the house. But the back door is open, and the little one gets into the pool. Ellen offers a nightmare I never heard; in her class, Michael vividly described a four-year-old's progress into the closet, into the dry cleaner's plastic bag, and her death by asphyxiation—discovered by her parents hours later. They meant well, all parents do, but every other minute there is danger. Brain damage. Death.

Or maybe you'll be lucky. You'll have a neighbor who knows CPR. Maybe you'll know CPR (having taken this course). So the baby can be kept alive until the paramedics get there. Michael can describe the paddles on the chest that bring drowning children, sometimes, back. His descriptions take us to the doors of death and beyond; our insides are shrieking.

Oh, God, we'll be so careful!!

Subversively, I feel like rushing home to make sure that no pool has been built within a mile of our apartment. But leaving would mean that I'd miss the lifesaving techniques and safety checklist that Michael holds the key to. I forget that the Red Cross course I took after Emma's birth was rather pleasant. (And cheaper.) I forget my name, my Social Security number. I reassure myself that they are written on pieces of paper somewhere, should I need to refresh my memory when the class finally ends.

Michael then explains that paper is hazardous, too. Yes: candy wrapper, newsprint, the price tag on your pants. He tells us about the well-meaning parent who saw his baby put a little piece of paper in his mouth. What would you do? This parent tried to get it out of the baby's mouth, but maybe it only went in farther, and *he didn't know what to do next.*

We are now in full-performance throttle. The class is listening, a bunch of suits and silk dresses topped by pale heads with mouths agape as though hoping for Michael's—what?—his Kiss of Life, what else? The poor pregnant women ("They're still terrified of *having* the baby," says Donna) stare balefully at their teacher. Stockholm syndrome has long since taken over, and he is our hero, our leader, our star. "They're ready to have the baby adopted," adds Donna. Preferably by him—after all, he was a paramedic.

A part of me rebels, as it tends to. Though forbidden to take notes (later, there are handouts, and books for sale), I madly scribble down his next phrase: "The [paper-swallowing] kid is gray—he's making high-pitched crowing noises!"

So are we. We are frightened, we are making high-pitched noises, we vow to remove all paper from our homes. But it's too late for the baby in the anecdote, which he has told us really happened, not far from where we are now sitting. Rushed to the emergency room by his an-guished father, the child died before he even got there.

"Another time," another story goes, "a kid climbed onto the stove, a hot stove, with a pan of boiling water on it—"

No, Michael, no!

And so it goes for hours, with the pregnant members of the audi-ence unable to leave for fear of missing something, and wincing at the prospect of bearing a child so perishable that the slightest thing can and surely will kill him. Audience is what we all are, captive to Michael's knowledge, for we have paid forty-five dollars a head. The book is an extra fifteen dollars, but we will pay it—we will pay anything. If life is so precious, I hope someone, somewhere, is offering this information gratis, and graciously.

I am later caught still jotting notes. Michael tells me sharply that I can "get" the book later. That I must listen if I want my child to remain safe and alive.

I'll take two books, a pennant, and a T-shirt!

I also learn that:

Pacifiers are not to be trusted. You put one in your baby's mouth. You go to sleep. Baby goes to sleep. He vomits. You are asleep, so you don't know. (Michael seems to suggest that new parents oughtn't to sleep too much—in this, he is in cahoots with nature.) The pacifier has made the vomit choke him better, faster, more permanently.

Since babies do vomit a lot, with pacifier or not, you must always monitor your baby for forty-five minutes after each feeding. (In fact, for the next three years, keep tuned to the monitor in his room: You do have one, don't you?) During the first months, you ought to sit vigilantly by the bedside, alert. Perhaps you could set up camp in the nursery, toothpicks propping your lids. But so be it: You want your kid to live, don't you? *I CAN'T HEAR YOU!*

"You'd have to be a superhuman to do it all," admits Donna, still approvingly. "But it's better than being blind to safety."

Sleeping parents are indeed blind. But be careful that your eyelid-propping toothpicks do not choke him, for Baby can choke on everything. Your earrings, the fuzz on his teddy, the strings on his hood. Do not trust the buttons on his clothing, the bumper ties, the mobile, hats that fasten at the neck. Do not put any blanket on him that does not have holes in it. Michael does not believe that sudden infant death is such a mystery. He suggests: no blankets without air holes, no pacifiers in bed, no bottles of water in bed, no liquid of any kind given to a child lying down. In England, he says, mattresses have holes in them, to drain the vomit. (So that's why the country has that funny warm-sour-milk smell.)

Baby can still be killed, though. Killed by that chest of drawers that you did not fasten to the wall. So he pulled it over himself, and it crushed him. Killed by the television set that you carelessly left plugged in (I'm not sure of the exact scenario). Killed by the French doors, which had glass in them—he walked right into them and hemorrhaged. Killed by that Band-Aid you put on him—he swallowed, or tried to swallow, it. Killed by the Fisher-Price Little People you bought for your older child. Killed by the taxi ride, since the taxi had no seat belt and you did not use a car seat. (Michael recommends that car seats be placed in the center of the backseat—fine if you have only one child. For those with more than one, choosing who gets the middle starts to become a variant of Sophie's choice.)

Dead babies everywhere, and you killed them, Mom and Dad.

Should they live beyond early infancy, Michael continues, do not feed any child under two or three a raisin, popcorn, more than a shred of chicken at a time. In fact, until your child has every molar in, better stick to the soft, mushy diet.

That, basically, concludes the lecture. We practice CPR and the Heimlich on dolls that are surprisingly lifelike—or, to my mind at that point—deathlike. Their arms hang limply, and though we breathe into and thump their tiny chests, no answering breath is heard, no eyelids flutter.

We wobble out, buy the book, and go home—each rushing to the respective bedsides of our girl and boy, sure to find another corpse. Miraculously, they are alive and breathing! We have never so appreciated life over death before; now, it threatens to become a frequent, fretful calculation. But Michael would say he has bettered our odds, and he has. "I'll never forget him," says Sue, who thinks he's "fabulous." *No* one could forget him.

My husband tries to turn this all into a joke, so that we can sleep. We make up our own dire scenarios:

Paul's: A guy in the grocery store takes the bottom can of cling peaches from a pyramid display and is crushed to death.

Mine: A woman goes to the hairdresser. She gets a nice cut and is happy, but one hair is askew. The hairdresser sprays the hair, not realizing that someone has just turned up the air-conditioning and that the vent is right near her. She is asphyxiated.

All night we have nightmares. We dream of Michael being on the scene when our children are in danger. We realize he will turn us into cautionary anecdotes for his next class. Is that good, though? A form of immortality?

We dream, too, of a safety catalog that has been coming to us (and, I suspect, all new parents) by mail. It contains drawer latches, table-

edge cushions, table-corner cushions, VCR locks, socket locks, cord short-
eners, appliance latches, potty locks, bathtub thermometers, door stop-
pers, stroller bumpers, carbon-monoxide detectors, and nontoxic Bear
Bath, "which safely cleans stuffed toys." We had not realized that all
other methods of cleaning stuffed toys were so hazardous.

Another dream is prompted by a recent article in the paper that
described another safety catalog, offering the personal services of a safety
expert, who would visit our home and show us where we are about to
go tragically wrong. These "home-safety parties," as they are oxymoroni-
cally called (for safety is no party), include "a room-by-room child-
proofing plan"—free if you hire the company to install the suggested
safety products.

Our safety dreams, being the dreams of Chicken Little, are not
entirely restorative. We wake up early, and we wake up groggy. Groggy
parents equal danger, for we are less vigilant, due to the overflow of
adrenaline during CPR class and the night that followed.

Still, I am alert enough to notice an article, the very next day, in
our paper of record, which talks about serving toddlers their finger food.
Like most literature on the subject, this article okays breads, cooked vege-
tables, and other assorted edibles. It does not seem to know—as do
Michael and his disciples—that anything more solid than lumpless
Maypo is a one-way ticket to Valhalla.

Even if you do grind everything, of course, most of what you are
grinding is polluted by the worst pesticides, as the media will tell you.
So worry, as per the next chapter.

FIFTEEN

WHEREIN BABY NEEDS ORGANIC, HOME-CRUSHED GRUB

Recently, food was perceived to be one more thing that could kill your child. Specifically, a mass alarm arose about pesticides. Veteran parents knew that Junior loved scarfing Twinkies at his friends' houses. They were loose about the organic brown-rice requirement, and did not get especially bothered by the fact that fruit orchards were sprayed against mites and mold. But new parents, still cradling their sucklings, began to feel a small hysterical ripple of fear.

It was growing knowledge that the apple a day that kept the doctors away could actually be laced with poison.

Cancer, said the Environmental Protection Agency, spurring new-parent paranoia. And not only in the apple, but in cherries, grapes, and peanuts. Cancer without and cancer within, and you can't wash it off, peel it, or boil it away.

This led to a fairly large grass-roots movement, spearheaded by celebrities and given airtime by *60 Minutes,* to banish Alar, the most notorious of the pesticides in use. Meant to preserve the *appearance* of the apple, Alar seemed an especially easy villain—it turned the fruit into the poisoned pippin given to Snow White with the wheedling "Isn't it red? Isn't it shiny?"

In the story's substratum lay the suspicion that Mother Earth and her children were being done in by some vast uncaring conglomerate, and that the latter should be stopped, or at least stymied, by a mothers' revolution.

It was: Alar was banned, and recent stories report no loss of love for apples in the American diet.

Still, the Alar kerfuffle led to a growing fascination with what goes into babies' mouths. And thus, inevitably, it also led to a proliferation of courses on how to prepare fresh (if not organic), homemade (if not home-grown) meals for the toothless consumer.

These courses typically require that grown women sit in a room and sample baby food. (Men's food-making buttons are not so easily pushed.) It tastes, as you might expect, rather bland. Then the teacher gives the women a taste of some real home-cooked carrot, or applesauce. Much better! Then recipes are introduced, step by step. Here is an example: Take one turnip. Wash carefully, scrubbing away all pesticides. Cook it until soft. Mash until mushy. Serve. Floss. (There are several of these courses in most cities; women who used to order Chinese every night sob quietly into their notebooks.)

As my mother would say, for this you went to college?

No, I went to college to learn that the food issue is more potent than the odd Alar hysteria, than the mush-making classes, than even the organic produce, raw and jarred, that mothers are buying their kids. What is important, as I see it, is the feeling one has that one is *nourishing* one's child, body and soul.

We are talking about atmosphere, ambience. Does the family eat together? Happily? Do the children associate eating with the taste, company, and fullness, or with force-feeding and plate-cleaning? Do you have a suspicion that your child's gastrointestinals affect your own? Do you push meals at your balking two-year-old? Failing, do you feel undone?

Three times a day, we are back to that magical table, either letting baby decide what nourishes him (having given him some reasonable options), or lecturing, threatening, and bribing. Studies say that young children will not willfully starve themselves, that they take in roughly the same amount of calories each day, even though they may eat very little at one meal and a great deal at another. The two-year-old's refusal to sit down for breakfast will thus probably not lead to mental defects, leading ultimately to dismissal from—or failure to get into—Harvard.

But somehow, for some of us, the kid's refusal to swallow what we put before him seems the ultimate rebellion. See James Dobson's *The Strong-Willed Child*, for instance, in which the author approvingly describes one father's response to "willful defiance" (a characteristic, we learn, of children): He threatens his son with "a spanking he would never forget" if he doesn't sit down and finish Mom's good home-cooking.

Buttoned lips are particularly vexatious if we've spent hours shopping for the precisely right organic apple, not too shiny (no wax), but not too dented, either. A small bit of Maine mud, but no wormholes, please. We've toted those tree-ripe conkers home in our little cotton-net bag. Then we've spent another eon by the stove, boiling that apple. We've mashed it to bits. No wonder we feel miffed when Mr. Two-Teeth throws it at the wall.

This is precisely why, for the first months of solid feeding, I browse through the jarred section. The care I take—having eliminated those with sugar and cornstarch and other assorted non-nutrients—is to see that the meal is pleasant. I put on some Raffi. I let the kids play with their food. My infant son moisturizes his hair; my daughter constructs moats. I offer with an eclecticism that does not, however, include Froot Loops and/or Jell-O, those staples of our own innocent-but-ignorant pasts.

At certain meals, my children eat breathlessly, soundlessly, pausing only to extend a mute hand for more. At others, they are as abstemious as Park Avenue lunchers. It all evens out, as do our varied temperaments.

I sound venerable, but it took ages to realize this principle. Once my daughter, at two, figured out that it bugged me if she had no breakfast, she was determined not to have it. I did not know that by three she'd be touchingly begging for more organic cornballs, every morning, precisely at half past seven. But at two, no amount of cajoling ("We have tayberry jam, hon!") no amount of threatening ("No breakfast after nine, hon!"—note forced "hon"), no amount of teasing ("Gabriel and I are having such a good breakfast here!"—total lie, as he was eating baby food from a jar, and I was squeezing it out of his hair), could induce the child to park before the matinal trough.

I thought of forcing her into the high chair—many mothers advised this, but to me it smacked (pun intended) of the James Dobson school. Remember, he is the one whose response to the fierce toddler will is to "give him one swat on the legs with a small switch" to "confirm your leadership." No switch swatter, I still felt awful hauling a kicking child into a chair and trying to make her stay, even though she sometimes did stay, and even eat. My second approach was more difficult. It involved asking myself why I felt that she had to eat upon waking (a time, I remembered, when I used to have no appetite). Finally, I tried not to care too much, one way or the other. I knew she wouldn't starve, and was more concerned, as I was when first nursing, that her attitude toward life, and food, be easygoing.

I suppose you think that I'll say she then took breakfast. Yes and no. She did when she was hungry. She didn't when she wasn't. I started to permit a cup of dry cereal in front of *Sesame Street,* which gave me the opportunity to stay in the kitchen and feed Gabriel. Snack-time was just around the corner, ten o'clock to be precise, during which rice cake and juice would be served in the kitchen. This somehow saved both our prides. She'd never been so hungry.

A bit of hunger is the best cook, they say.

Another good cooking tip might be the fact that I'd sit with her for snack. Gabriel was by now napping. Emma and I could sit in the kitchen, companionably, and eat together. She with her rice cake and juice, I with mine. A year later, I still try to eat as many meals together with her as I can. Because she's good fun at the table, and so am I. Now.

That's what I learned from all those courses about how to feed your child.

SIXTEEN

ROCKING WITH BABY

Gymboree and the like have clued you in to baby's physical needs. Now, you must reckon with the child's need for music. Luckily (or not), the children's music industry increased by over 50 percent in 1991 alone, to $300 million.

My friend horrified me with the tale that her three-year-old wouldn't "let" her play any of her own tapes. Yes, Mozart and Bach are taboo chez this child. Mother *must* play the three-year-old's tapes—or face the consequences, i.e., high-pitched whining, deafening volume, boring repetition of the same flat phrases. Well, sometimes those tapes themselves carry similar consequences.

A little background on how things get out of hand in Musical Babyland.

In the beginning, there was rock and roll, heavy and hot, and you fell in love, got married, and conceived. Or maybe it was Mozart or Bach, and you dreamed rose-window dreams, and fell in love, got married, and conceived. Or was it Tin Pan Alley, was it jazz, that opened your hormonals to the sweet willy-nilly?

There is a baby in your house now. And you, old music-lover, are wondering what to put on the tape deck. There will be pitfalls, you know; much kiddie fare is yuck. If you're not very, very careful, your house will sound like Romper Room—and you will lose your temper and your style.

There are, of course, adult sounds that do well for little ears. Chopin and Sade and oddly, Philip Glass, do well for Emma. Sophie, my friend's child, loves "The Moonshine Lullaby" from *Annie Get Your Gun,* as sung by either La Merman or her own mother, Simone ("I belt it out," says Simone. "She seems to like it!") And some adult artists have made tapes for children, such as *Peter, Paul and Mommy.*

Is there a way to escape the false, the slick, and the condescending in the children's music world itself? There is. There are listenable tapes now available. Listenable to you, that is. In fact, there are many. You will wonder, Where have they been all my life? Your child won't have to ask that question: She *will* have had the tape all her life.

1. The Essential

Number one on my list, your list, anyone's list, seems to be Raffi (one name, like Prince, Madonna, and Liberace). Raffi, like many great contemporary children's artists, hails from Canada, where the snow is deep and the moose run free. Snow and moose notwithstanding, Raffi is an international superstar; even *The Wall Street Journal* has given him some profile. There is a reason for this.

Unlike some other performers in this field, Raffi doesn't seem to pump himself up for children's entertainment. Not for him is that surly-making, fake Uncle Bob, "Hi, kiddies!" tone. His manner is relaxed, conversational, unshowy. Raffi is a folksy sort of guy, bearded and interestingly shod. At the same time, the songs have emotional underpinnings—contentment, reflection, mischief, joy. And he's musically sophisticated, too, not only in the variety of material (most of which is original), but in the phrasing and the orchestration. Listen to his bluegrass adaptation of "This Old Man" on the popular *Baby Beluga* tape. Then imagine the kitschy ways it could have been recorded.

Through graceful transitions within a single album, from one musical idiom to another, from Japanese to calypso to Gallic (some songs are French-Canadian), Raffi expresses his uncorny vision of a world united by children, love, and music. Try his exquisite *One Light, One Sun* album. In "Like You and Me," one selection from that album, Raffi names children from all parts of the globe; his essence is distilled in 120 moving seconds.

Raffi's complexity seems to emerge from his experiences, both as an artist and as a human being. Surprisingly, this man whose records tend to go beyond platinum (indicating a sale of more than 100,000 records in Canada alone) is shy, childless, and has spent a good part of his adult years struggling with professional disappointment.

Born in Cairo about forty years ago to affluent Armenian parents, Raffi Cavoukian moved to Toronto with his family when he was ten. There, he and his father (a well-known photographer) sang together in the Armenian church choir. By the sixties, Raffi made another move: Dropping out of college, he began crossing Canada with his guitar.

In 1975, he formed his own label, aptly named Troubadour, and recorded his first album, *Good Luck Boy,* a collection of his folk songs. The misnamed album sold only two thousand copies, and a year later Raffi hung up his guitar.

Around this seemingly infelicitous time, however, he married Debi Pike, his high school sweetheart. In doing so, he gained not only a supportive wife but a mother-in-law who taught nursery school.

Daphne Pike had the brainy idea that Raffi should play some songs for her charges. Raffi knew nothing about children and even less about their music. When he listened to the few children's albums that were available at the time, he was appalled and bored. When he finally dived in, he came up with gold—a new perspective and a new career.

A four-thousand-dollar loan later, Raffi (with the help of musician-producer Ken Whitely) recorded his premier album for children, *Singable Songs for the Very Young.* He chose not to charge the conventional $2.98 that other children's albums cost, but rather to match the product's price—and quality—to that of adult fare. (A wise tactic, as it happened.) Next, he took a pile of records, loaded them into his car, and drove from store to store, asking only that the owner play them so that shoppers could hear. Complying, store owners found that they could not keep the music in stock. Raffi, at last, was a hit, and the debut album has become a classic.

The fairy tale doesn't quite end there. The following year, along with *More Singable Songs,* Raffi tested the mainstream market yet again with a record bearing the deliberately named *Adult Entertainment.* Due perhaps to its ambiguously suggestive title, the album sold few copies. Raffi renamed his record *Lovelight:* still no go. In 1978, he went back to making music devoted to children.

Devotion is the word, and it is mutual. In concert, Raffi holds his arms out like a swami, and children (mostly aged three to eight) swarm forward, dancing. They know the music and they know the words. They love the man. When they grow up, they want to have warm, philosophical eyes and a close-cropped beard, just like his.

FOOTNOTE TO RAFFI: Be aware of Raffi wannabes, a tribute to his popularity. Most of them are, in fact, pretty good. Try Willie Sterba (*Chickens in My Hair*), Frank Capelli (*You Wanna Be a Duck?*) or Fred Penner (*A House for Me*). They do what Raffi does—alternate folk with humor, whole-wheat/whole-earth sentiment, and funk, though perhaps not quite as well.

Late postscript: Sadly, Raffi is still making attempts to win the adult market. He has recently announced that he would no longer create children's music (although MCA Records will distribute his existing collection). His new album, *Evergreen, Everblue,* is dedicated to ecological concerns. Though it is sold in children's shops, there is a liner note from Raffi that indicates crossover ambitions: "I believe that we can rescue our beleaguered planet only through a change of heart and mind. My new music celebrates our power to act together to preserve the beauty and bounty of the Earth for our children's future. *This album is different*—a musical call to action and commitment *for all of us old enough to make a difference* [italics mine]."

Oh, Raffi, what would your real fans think if they could read this? Can't they make a difference? (My daughter is already worrying about litter on Mother Earth's face.)

My husband thinks it's terrible that a man with such a gift for entertaining children has to keep thinking that it's not a "real" talent, that he must prove himself in the "real," i.e., the adult, world. Nor does he think that Raffi has the Dylanesque (Bob or Thomas) gifts of adult-market folk heroes. Check out the lyrics of the title song, "Evergreen, Everblue." They seem as gawky and clichéd as those liner notes above, using flat-footed phrases like "at this point in time."

"At this point in time," we'd like to see Raffi come back to the tiny stage and stay there. Perhaps he, like us parents, is afraid that he's being stereotyped into his role, a "mere" children's entertainer. This is upsetting for the kids and the parents who love him. Does Raffi think childhood's not legit?

2. The Talented

Rory is an up-and-coming female artist who boldly says *she* will be the next Raffi. (She can already lay claim to the female Raffi title.) To someone who has listened to the gang of male wannabes, Rory is a standout in terms of personality, versatility, and musicianship. (Try her *I'm a Kid*.) She is also a standout in her gender: Shari Lewis notwithstanding, the children's music business, like the music business in general (but unlike the child-rearing "business," i.e. parenthood), seems to be a man's domain.

Sharon, Lois and Bram, are, indeed, two-thirds female. But they got on my nerves at first. They seemed so relentlessly up, like Partridges or Archies! And pushy, too: Kids, everybody clap!

But wait. This bunch of Canadians grew on me; they'll grow on you. First of all, you can dance to them: If you have a young one, scoop him up, take his left hand in your right, and twirl for all you're worth (makes 'em chuckle). This trio, by the way, is my children's favorite. Their energy reliably makes Emma display the multitoothed smile, both top and bottom, and Gabriel give me the gummy beam that melts Mommy. You can watch 'em on TV, too.

Rosenshontz are witty in a way that older kids (that is, older than three) may like. I'm told that this group is the one that takes over when Raffi's infinite variety (and infinite whole wheatness) begins to grow stale. *Tickles You* and *Rock 'n' Roll Teddy Bear* are good examples.

At first you may shun Paul Strausman's *Camels, Cats and Rainbows*, with its misleading fey title. You might believe that you'd have to wear rose quartz and play the wind chimes to get anything out of it. But no. This is an album you can listen to over and over. (Perhaps I've been hypnotized into liking it.) Strausman has a voice as nice as Raffi's, by the way.

Eric Nagler is something else. A jug-band-playing, footstompin' hero, transplanted to—where else?—Canada, where he seems to thrive. (He's a friend of Sharon, Lois and Bram.) *Fiddle Up a Tune* is wild and cathartic. In my house, the tape is ripped to ribbons, the product, I think, of musical euphoria.

Hap Palmer is now famous for his videos, discussed in the next chapter. His slant is children's small, real-life victories, depicted in songs like "I Can Put My Clothes On by Myself." Children can start listening to these simple (and addictive) ditties at birth, and every month, they'll get more out of them in terms of recognition and identification. Try *Baby Songs, More Baby Songs,* and the recently released *Even More Baby Songs.* Indeed, there can never be enough Baby Songs.

Tom Glazer is the classic example of the soft-voiced man with the acoustic guitar (strum, strum, strum), but the man has been around for over four decades, so let's show a little respect and put on his *Music for Ones and Twos.* Better yet, ask the baby-sitter to try it—and run from the house. Flee.

This represents a musical bridge to the next category.

3. The Fairly Horrible

Anything by Wee Sing (the wee name itself is a giveaway) is guaranteed to be precious and didactic ("And *then* what did he say?"). Some listeners might enjoy the trip through London Towne (featured on *Wee Sing Nursery Rhymes and Lullabies*) in which, parading through the English capital, we encounter the likes of Jack Horner and Old King Cole. I found myself glumly yearning for a trip to the Tower.

Baby Farm Animals: Ditto.

Favorite Animal Songs, sung by opera singer Francine Lancaster—oh, please.

(The above three are intended for the very young, but you cannot be young enough.)

The music of Sarah Pirtle (*Two Hands Hold the Earth*) might belong to a group of tapes that were recorded during one of Shirley MacLaine's lifetimes on Atlantis. Très dewy and gooey.

The bottom line is that childhood is neither a state of mental retardation nor emotional anemia. But don't go to extremes and feel you have to buy the cacophonous likes of Barry Louis Polisar's *My Brother Thinks He's a Banana, and Other Provocative Songs for Children.* In this genre, throwing up is thought to be a hoot. (Examples of the Polisar wit: In a song called "My Name is Hiram Lipshlitz," the joke is that it's better to be "a Smith or Jones.") This tuneless fellow (whose voice is a seamless whine) is quite popular, by the way. To my mind, the stuff sounds like rap for baby psychopaths.

4. The Tranquil

There are many wonderful lullaby tapes, and they are useful in parental lives. I love *Lullaby Magic* (I and II), sung by the clear yet slightly throb-voiced Joanie Bartels. (Her *Bathtime Magic* and *Silly Songs* are also pleasers.) Either of Bartel's lullaby tapes is a classic, but if forced to pick one, I'd take the first, with its soft, serious rendition of "Wynken Blynken and Nod."

Try also *A Child's Gift of Lullabies*, which begins with a diapason of notes, tossed forth like a veil of gold: It captures you in a fragile, trembling web of melody. Mike Rowland's *Fairy Ring*, voiceless, orchestral, and magical, evokes Lancelot (or Lady Lovelylocks), and Synchestra's *Mother Earth's Lullaby*, while not everyone's cup of chamomile tea, is mesmerizing. Zenlike in its monotony (like breathing), this wise-fool music can be therapeutically lulling to both parent and child. It evokes, for me, the meditative, curative, unpetty-paced sound of the sea.

Dose yourself cautiously.

Some of this music is so powerful that it may make you weep and weep. At least *I* wept, but then, I was just a few weeks postpartum with my first child when I started tuning in. The baby didn't sleep much, either. Now that we're older and we have another baby in the house, we're sophisticated.

So now my two babies sail off on a river of crystal light, into a sea of dew. And my husband and I kick back and relax.

SEVENTEEN

VIDEO ROCKING

A t some point, you will run out of things to do with and say to your baby, and when the child-psychiatry experts are not watching, you will evilly plop him in front of the television.

You may feel guilty about besmirching your child with the vile fare that is on television. Even *Sesame Street,* say some, is too fast-paced, especially for the neonate. Disney and Nickelodeon have commercials, which to my mind vitiate completely any positive things observed in the surrounding program. So perhaps, like me, you will buy or rent a video.

Relax: Sit back for the first time in months. You are, after all, the one who persistently thought of plopping a baby in front of the tube. If Baby is your child genetically, he is likely to be transfixed. (If you do not yourself own a television, you will not be able to carry out the converse experiment.)

I began with Hap Palmer's video *Baby Songs,* and bless her, my Emma is still watching them. At first I think what appealed to her was simply the motion, the occasional ball bouncing, duck waddling, streamer streaming.

Eventually, she began to get the developmental points that Palmer is making: What happens when Mommy leaves? She comes back. ("She never would forget me.") Emma also liked a ditty called "Walking." The song is simply a description of how babies learn this difficult task, which involves falling on your bottom quite a lot. After hearing it over and over, however, I think it emerges as a good metaphor for any serious undertaking. The toilet-training ditty "Today I Took My Diapers Off" is also popular with two-year-olds ("I never felt so free"), but I am still working on the metaphorical aspects. The film features a little girl strutting around in jeans, and then a bathing suit, proud that what you see is all her, unpadded. Perhaps some association could be made to early feminist bra-burning. I'm not sure.

The Disney-studio Pooh tapes are so incredibly well made that even my English mother-in-law found nothing in them to shame Milne. Managing not to vulgarize the bear of little brain and his woodland pals, Disney has added subtle songs to the picture and text. Even the *New Adventures of Winnie the Pooh,* which you might imagine to be neon-crass, have their charm, which largely resides in the music.

The more pervasive Disney Sing-Along song tapes feature highlights, à la MTV, from their various movies, complete with subtitled lyrics and the occasional bouncing ball. These aren't bad, though Disney does seem to pad its movies with noisy ads for other things you ought to get. I like the one called *Fun with Music,* which seems never to end, and features the loopy narration of Professor Ludwig Von Drake.

None of the above is likely to bore Mom and Dad, even after a thousand viewings, which there will be.

I cannot say the same for two computer-imaged tapes that are obtainable through the yuppier (black/white mobile-type) catalogs, and the occasional overpriced baby-gear boutique.

The first, *Infastastic,* has coarse computer images that are practically static, accompanied by tinny, wordless renditions of songs like "Hush Little Baby" and "This Old Man." (Should you wish to sing along—your voice will add immeasurably to the musical texture—the lyrics are included, in a little handout.)

While watching this video, I had a great epiphany: the melody of "Twinkle, Twinkle" and the "Alphabet Song" are the same! I was unable, however, to draw any useful lesson from this knowledge, other than that children tend to love both songs, as well as "Baa, Baa, Black Sheep," which also has the same tune but somehow didn't make it to this tape.

The other computer-image tape, one my daughter calls "Mr. Bobo," is the brainchild of a researcher called Dr. Marshall Haith, who claims to have studied what little babies like for about twenty years. Despite this intimacy with the infantile attention span, Dr. Haith precedes the tape proper with a prolonged lecture about his methodology and goals. Another epiphany: My Gabriel *was* intrigued by the introductory lecture, as much as by what followed. This despite the fact that Dr. Haith's presentation consists of a seated professorial man, himself, talking, with one or two turns back and forth to this camera and that.

Dr. Haith tells us, at length, that babies like color, contrast, change, and movement. Not only that, they "form expectations for where an object will reappear after it's disappeared," and they like to relate sights and sounds. "These principles of early perception," he reassures us, lead to the visual and aural presentations to follow.

SO SHOW US SOMETHING ALREADY!

Not yet.

"Thus," he continues, "your baby will be able to practice several developing skills with this video," i.e., discriminating, tracking, forming expectations, and finding the relations between sights and sounds.

Sounds very scientific, so Dr. Haith explains the fun principle. This is where the expert stands back and sort of chides parents for buying the very thing he has been promoting, for being somehow "led to believe that they must do special things, or buy special products, to make their babies develop faster, better." His suggestion, offered on this very tape (which has cost about twenty dollars)? "Relax."

Does that mean get a refund?

No.

He goes on to say that no special benefits will occur, just baby's pleasure in exercising his perceptual skills.

No puritan, I nevertheless wonder whether the pleasure in exercising those skills couldn't be achieved in the real world, without the benefit of electrical devices.

In a way, it can't be. Gabriel goes gaga for Bobo. (He's pretty keen on *Infantastic,* too.) Grinning, laughing, shouting at the screen, whipping his head around when I attempt to take him out of the room, straining for another glimpse of those much-researched images. Is this good? Yeah, I guess so.

This leaves me to wonder whether some of these child experts actually might know a thing or two.

A distressing thought. Does this mean there are other worthies out there, items to be bought and programs to follow?

Of which more in the next chapter.

EIGHTEEN

WHEREIN BABY CANNOT BE SMART ENOUGH OR STIMULATED ENOUGH

Subsection A: Toys for Baby

"Now it's possible to make certain your baby has the right toys at the right time."

Thank goodness I got this *solicitation* in time!

This is the bold-faced, red-colored copy on a brochure for a certain well-known brand of "Child Development Toys" (hereinafter to be referred to, iconoclastically, as merely "toys"), once sponsored by the Johnson and Johnson company, and now by a popular parents' magazine, who also back a "free" magazine put out by Pampers.

Need it be said that that magazine will probably never do an article in which the value of toy clubs—or Pampers—will be questioned?

Never mind. You have *Mothering Heights,* Faithful Reader, and will not want for the skeptical champion.

So skeptical was I that shortly after Gabriel's birth I signed up for the club, hoping to stimulate my new son and avoid his imminent retardation. And this despite the fact that I should have known better. During my daughter's infancy, I had purchased one of the famous toys (now discontinued), an impressive rattle. Emma promptly whacked herself on the head with it and let out a horrible bawl. They no longer sell that particular rattle, I noticed, but the one they do sell is just as big. Bigger.

Speaking of big: In the sales pitch that I received in the mail, one line stood out: "You needn't worry that the toys were designed to be attractive to you, rather than helpful for your baby." Funny they should mention that. The toys are, indeed, big enough for the adult hand, and then some. They are almost as big as my son's arm. Even the photo of the new rattle is eye-filling. Clear Rattle, as it is called, is BIG in the same savory way that cornflakes, or Doggie Treats, are sometimes portrayed to the wide-eyed human.

By the way, each toy comes accompanied with a passel of offers for other wonderful products Mom can buy (a Bonding Bonus!). For example: a free eight-by-ten of baby from the JC Penney Portrait Studio; a Disney Book Club brochure; an offer for the Dr. Seuss Book Club; and—my favorite—Joy Berry's infamous (to me; more later) book club, Help Me Be Good, ("turn naughty into nice") which begins with the "free" title, geared for the young child, called "Disobeying."

It's reasonable to assume that a household that requires professional counsel on how to play will soon be requiring professional counsel on how to act morally in a complex world.

Lesson One should be: Don't exploit parent's fears and weaknesses. But it isn't.

And now, back to our regularly scheduled program.

THE CLEAR RATTLE SAGA

Clear Rattle is accompanied by an ominous little blue card. It says: IMPORTANT PLAY INFORMATION ABOUT CLEAR RATTLE.

The important play information is this: While Clear Rattle (or simply "rattle" to its friends) *is* designed with an eye to maximum play benefits for both newborns and older babies, in the case of a baby under *five months old* (this despite the fact that the toy is marketed for the two- to four-monther), "you, the parent" must "stimulate your baby's emerging senses of sight and sound, as illustrated in the accompanying Play and Learning (TM) Guide."

Reading between the lines, one might guess that quite a few babies have been bonking and bawling with this rattle, leaving their parents no choice but to pen malicious letters to the toy company. (I was too busy administering cold compresses to my firstborn.) With the aid of this little blue card (at about two inches by three, far smaller than Clear Rattle), you have been warned. But given the length of the toy, its weight on the far end (though lighter than its predecessor), and the weakness of the infantile arm, I would not leave a child alone with it until he can spell out "throbbing head lump."

The Play and Learning (TM) Guide that comes with the toys is similarly big and impressive (at seventeen pages, longer than many term papers). Its complexity derives from the fact that the uses of Clear Rattle change with the age of your child—*never losing play value!!!*

When Baby is newborn to two months, you can begin showing her "some features of her new toy." Example:

"Hold Clear Rattle near you baby's eyes so she can explore it. Shake it gently so she can hear the sounds."

As my mother would say, for this you need a booklet?

Wait, Mom, wait. They're only getting started.

You are then instructed to put your child on her back and move Clear Rattle slowly from one side of her head to the other. This experience, which will be followed by the movement of your baby's eyes, is called "tracking," which, if you know Bobo, you already know plenty about. The Guide tells you that your child might even "turn her head to keep the toy in view," all in order to "practice focussing and coordinated eye movements."

The Guide does not tell you that tracking can also be practiced with the parent's own hand, a bookmark, a runcible spoon, and certainly with the generic Pathmark phone ($2.99) which Gabriel instantly seemed to prefer to Clear Rattle.

When Baby is two to four months, you are supposed to hold Clear Rattle above her chest and let her bat at it. Or—"new game!"—hold it steady and encourage baby to reach for it. This will develop eye-hand coordination as well as interfamilial tension, should the latter not develop as described in the guide.

At four to six months your baby's on his own. *He can hold Clear Rattle.* Most babies, burbles the Guide, will try mouthing it: "Babies we tested enjoyed mouthing the globe as much as the ring." Ooh-la-la. Then they add (protesting too much?) "Clear Rattle's slender handle and light weight make it easy to hold." But not before that crucial fifth month, remember.

Additional features? No problem.

Here is some "leg-exercising kicking fun." Put Baby on her back again. Place Clear Rattle over her feet. No action? Just "tap it against her foot a few times to get her started." Oh, we have ways to make baby play with Clear Rattle!

Skipping ahead to nine months, you are still not getting rid of Clear Rattle. Put Clear Rattle in a container (says the Guide), and shake the container a few times. Then ask Baby to find the rattle. The container, by the way, could be "a plastic food storage container," though the Guide offers a HINT that freezer containers or juice pitchers may be used instead of food-storage containers. The toy, face it, has the versatilty of a ball of string.

(Author's HINT: If you like, substitute any inanimate object—even that ball of string—for Clear Rattle. It will work just as well for both the shaking game and the finding game.)

The Guide takes you through the toddler years, offering IDEAS! that only add to the fun. (One involves the toddler marching around and making "music"—their quote marks—with the rattle.) The basic IDEA under all the IDEAS is simply this: You will be carting that toy around with you for the rest of your life—and you'd better start to like it.

Then the Guide gets technical. Historical information, including the "history of rattles" (from 2500 B.C. to Clear Rattle) is included. Did you know that "England's Queen Victoria" (I love the way they have to add "England's"—they're not taking *any* level of smarts for granted) gave two gold rattles to the Prince of Wales, when he was a baby, and then that baby, probably as a result of such stimulation, "later became Edward VIII"—of what country, you're asking? They tell you—"of England." The same thing could happen to your child, right here!

There is, they conclude, a *huge* connection between "historical rattles and their modern counterparts, such as Clear Rattle." Yes, "the core of Clear Rattle lies in ancient history." This is more than a toy. It is a historical, no, an *archaeological* artifact. I hope you and baby are getting all these play levels.

There is also a "Teachers' Corner." How many infants have teachers? Yours should. This specialized instruction section includes "teacher" saying to the baby, "Karen—where is your rattle? Can you find it?" (I tried this, but my son would not respond to the name of "Karen.")

Teacher, you can also play Sound Search when your baby is finally able to sit for his lesson. This is done by shaking the rattle off to the side, above, "or in other locations." This will improve her "sound-seeking skills" (so will Mom's speaking to her from another part of the room) and help "exercise her neck and torso muscles."

A section called "Wrap Up" makes the most practical suggestions. One: Take this toy—and others made by the same company—*whenever you go out*. With the accompaniment of Clear Rattle, Red Rings, Tracking Tube, and their appropriate Play and Learning (TM) Guides, you'll discover that such "planning results in more rewarding outings for everyone."

(Especially the toy company.)

Anonymous parents' tips are interspersed throughout the Guide. One mother describes the way her child takes Clear Rattle from one corner of the room to the other, as he crawls, adding that it makes "such a great sound when it hits the floor. I call him the choo choo train."

This is the sound of a person with little to do—not because he or she has taken the time to name her child's activity "choo choo train" (and I, personally, don't see the connection), but because she has written to the staff of the Play and Learning (TM) Guide! If the writer lives, as I do, in an apartment building, the "great sound" of Clear Rattle smashing the floor with each lurch of Junior's hips will be superseded by the sound of the downstairs neighbor, sobbing.

My husband tells me that Gabriel cried the other morning. He had woken up to see his father brandishing Clear Rattle, intent on challenging play. Still, others have cried, in awe, upon viewing Everest. In time they master the mountain; the toy, as we have seen, remains a thing of (developmental) beauty forever.

The Guide backs the awesome claims with concrete data. Average playtime with Clear Rattle is 10.4 minutes as opposed to 6.4 minutes with Brand X rattle. An accompanying chart graphs the play duration, in minutes, by age, in months. Then the Guide analyzes these scientific findings:

"[N]o matter how delicately or clumsily a baby plays," it claims, you will get a veritable tympanic smorgasbord out of that rattle.

Author's IDEA: Determine if your baby is clumsy or delicate. If the former, feel ashamed. If the latter, feel proud. Brag. Write valedictory letters to the parent company.

Author's HINT: If your child, despite all your careful readings and teachings, and despite the fact that he is over five months old, as warned by the little blue card, keeps accidentally hitting himself on the head with Clear Rattle, remove toy from his sight and offer *Wiggle Worm,* for which he may now be developmentally ready.

THE WIGGLE WORM SAGA

A short saga (oxymoron?). Despite the dubious charms of Worm (the tail crackles, the head squeaks, etc.), my son hates the toy, whose eyes are on either side of its head, like a flounder. On to Red Rings, which is sure to be liked by Gabriel, as he likes balls, and Red Rings has one (though it did not make it into the toy's name). If Red Rings does not appeal, I intend to terminate membership.

THE RED RINGS SAGA

Red Rings is, as it's name implies, a bunch of rings, red, concentric, implying (to me at least) the solar system, in the center of which is that ball, jangling. According to the booklet, it can be chewed, banged, looked through, played peekaboo with, shaken, tracked, etc. There is no end to what you can do with the thing. The booklet, going I think too far, suggests that you and baby play tug-of-war with it. Perhaps the authors thought of that one in the wee hours, when they were getting testy with each other, not to mention with Red Rings. It is, however, a toy I have seen everywhere (it is even in the Baby Exercise video), and everywhere it has been played with what appears to be great enthusiasm.

Not at my house. Gabriel still prefers the generic Pathmark telephone rattle, and if not the telephone rattle, then the little helicopter rattle (by a less deluxe and far saner toy company, Discovery), and if not that, the little bear, Oatmeal, who squeaks. He will look at Red Rings, giving it the fair shot, the perfunctory shake, given to all toys that do not concuss him (and you know which toys I mean), but little more.

I should tell you though, I once had to terminate a phone conversation in order to rescue Gabriel from Red Rings. Trying to stop whipping his head with the toy, he got his arm stuck up to the pit in one of the Rings, and was despondent about their unappeasable, no-win nature. Valuable playtime was lost, too, and perhaps some affection for expensive playthings.

I am terminating membership. I am calling the 800 number and giving them the heave-ho that Gabriel, no Mike Tyson, cannot do for himself.

Subsection B: Brains by the Bookload

You absolutely must buy the following three books. One: *How to Teach Your Baby to Read,* by Glenn Doman. The cover of one edition features an infant staring at a flash card that says, surrealistically, HEAD; the other edition shows a little girl pointing to a flash card saying FOOT. Take your pick. Two: *How to Teach Your Baby Math* (by the same author), subtitled *The Gentle Revolution.* Three: (Baby should by now be counting along with you): *How to Have a Smarter Baby: The Infant Stimulation Program for Enhancing Your Baby's Natural Development,* by Dr. Susan Ludlington-Hoe (with Susan K. Golant). Take a moment to note how subtly the last intermingles the words "stimulation," "enhancement," and "program" with good old "natural development."

It's best to begin with the *Smarter Baby* book, as it covers the crucial prenatal learning months, often overlooked by busy parents-to-be. This book devotes quite a lot of pages to the stimulated, enhanced, programmed—but still naturally developing—fetus. There will still be time, after the baby is born, for those reading and math lessons.

Dr. Ludlington-Hoe advises us to make a prenatal tape of Mother's and Father's voices "to improve communicating to the fetal ear." Not *only* will such a tape, as described below, start your fetus pointing in the general direction of Cambridge, Massachusetts, and New Haven, Connecticut, but "consistent use of this tape may help in the bonding process."

A Bonding Bonus!

In the chapter called "A Rootin' Tootin' Tape," we see Dr. L-H directing an expectant couple, the Cornets, in their first IQ-raising move.

"First, they nicknamed their fetus. This . . . helped them (and will help you) recognize the fetus as a separate being—"

As opposed to a mere extension of parental narcissism.

Dr. L-H notes that "Cornet" means "horn," and since the Cornets didn't know if they were having a boy or a girl—clearly they had not followed Landrum Shettles and/or had sperm fractionation and/or CV testing—

"—they chose 'R.T.,' an abbreviation for 'Rootin' Tootin.'"

Judy Cornet's tape went like this:

"R.T., this is your mother speaking. I love you, R.T. R.T., this is your mother speaking. I can't wait for you to be born, R.T. I love you, R.T. R.T., this is your mother speaking."

R.T. says nothing. He is thinking, Get me outta here.

And mother's not finished:

"R.T., I'm going to read Mother Goose to you," she says, and then she does.

Judy's husband, Tom, is also quite the wag. His monologue to the fetus is similar to his wife's, but he makes the additional observation that he loves baby despite the hefty fees the OB/gyn is getting for labor and delivery.

Not to mention Dr. L-H's fee for tape-consultation.

The doctor continues, telling us that during the seventh month of the pregnancy the parents began playing the tape daily, putting "stereo headphones" on Judy's stomach, "near R.T.'s ears."

Assuming R.T. didn't skedaddle away from the noise, that is.

Proof of the tapes' value? It's obtained by videotape on R.T.'s birth date. R.T. is placed on his mother's chest right after he is born. He behaves normally. Then his father, who is "positioned" on the left, starts repeating key phrases, such as "R.T., this is your daddy speaking. I love you, R.T. My name is Tom. I love you, R.T."

Not enough, though, to quit calling you R.T.

The experts report that at the sound of his father's voice, little R.T. *"lifted his head and turned to the left to find the source of the familiar intonations!"* (their emphasis).

Clearly, the child was determined to find out the source of several months' nonstop annoyance.

As long as his father spoke, R.T. kept looking in his direction, turning his head when Tom moved. "[A]mid all the noise in that . . . delivery room, little R.T. was able to distinguish his father's voice and actually seek it out!"

As in, I'm gonna seek you out, I'm gonna find you, and you're gonna pay for what you done to me 'fore I was *born*.

So, concludes Dr. Ludlington-Hoe, talking to your fetus means you may be teaching, or—better yet—*"conditioning* him" to know your distinctive sound patterns.

There is more, much more, you can do to ensure your fetus's early conditioning. Most people would shy away from the epithet "Pavlovian," but Dr. L-H positively embraces it, as the next section, called "Of Pavlov and Parental Love," illustrates.

We are told of Ivan Pavlov, the nineteenth-century Russian scientist, and his approach to the training of animals. Every time Pavlov's dogs were fed, he rang a bell. Eventually, the poor animals learned to associate this sound with food, "and they salivated in response." When Pavlov rang the bell but did not give food, the dogs continued drooling in anticipation.

From this the author extrapolates that "yes . . . fetuses are capable of being *conditioned* long before they are born."

Pavlovian proof? Dr. L-H mentions scientific research with "a combination of vibrator and wooden clapper," to see if fetuses could be trained to respond. When the vibrator alone was placed across the maternal abdomen, "causing a gentle vibration within the womb," nothing happened. So researchers tried the clapper: "When the two pieces of wood slammed together, the fetuses moved in a startled way at the loud, unexpected noise."

Another Bonding Bonus!

The next step involved combining both vibrator and clapper. If you would like to repeat this procedure, combine the sound of the "clapper and five seconds of vibration with four minutes of rest time." Do this sixteen times, and you will find that most fetuses will react—i.e., move in a startled way—to the vibration alone. You, too, will conclude, as did the research team, that fetuses can be conditioned. (Yes, but what is being done for zygotes and lonely egg cells?)

There *is* more to be done in this field. Dr. L-H cites Dr. F. René Van de Carr, a Californian obstetrician, who asked a group of pregnant women to talk to their fetuses in a special way. They taped themselves laughing, or rather "saying 'Ha, ha, ha, ha . . .'" This "stylized laugh," as Van de Carr calls it, was played to the fetus daily during the last two months of gestation.

Nothing, says Dr. L-H, prepared Dr. Van de Carr for the newborns' reactions to this laughter: Many made distinct sounds, as early as four days after birth. Some parents even reported hearing their babies say "Haha . . . Haha . . . Haha. . . ."

Was this postpartum delirium (on the part of the parents)? More objective testing was needed.

Dr. Van de Carr attempted the technique on his own fetus, who, at one week after birth made laughing sounds.

Any parent—or scientist—would be tickled pink.

Hahahaha!

From this, Dr. Ludlington-Hoe concludes that language can be taught "sooner than we ever dreamed possible!"

Dr. Van de Carr has also created a prenatal program called the Prenatal University, which boasts over four hundred graduates.

Should you wish to develop your fetus's neuromuscular pathways (without enrolling him in Prenatal U), Dr. Van de Carr suggests that you:

"*Stroke* your fetus, and say, 'Stroke, I'm stroking you.'

"*Pat* your fetus and say, 'Pat, I'm patting you.' "

You are probably getting the gist here. Do the same with squeezing your fetus (whatever that means, and I shudder to think), and rubbing your fetus in little circles.

There is more. Dr. L-H cites a Dr. Anthony DeCasper, who recommends reading stories to the fetus. After sixteen mothers read *The Cat in the Hat* to their fetuses, the latter, when born, sucked very hard on the suckometer (a rigged pacifier) when the story was heard again.

You should also, she says, attempt an early introduction to classical music, naming the piece and composer before it is played (you don't want baby confusing Johann Strauss with Richard Strauss, God forbid).

Putting it all together, here is a sample mother's script of my own invention:

"Dudley, it's me again. Yes, mm-hmm. *Mater,* mother, *madre.* That's Spanish. Do you know Spanish? *Ti amo beaucoup* [*sic*], baby." (Repeat three times.)

"Dud, I'm going to sing. Would you like that? *Mucho?*"

(Sing "Besame Mucho.")

"Dudley, it's still Maman. You're so very special, and I mean that sincerely. Would you like me to sing 'Feelings' now?"

(Sing: "Feelings/Nothing more than feelings," etc . . .)

"Dudley, guess what! I bought shoes today. Ferragamo. Can you spell Ferragamo?

"Speaking of Italians, I'm gonna spin some *verismo* here for you. Don't you just love *Pagliacci?* You know, where the clown cries?

"Anyway, *ciao* for now."

Dr. L-H's mother, in the book's example, signs off with "I can't *wait* till I see you." Apparently not.

And who could wait when, after the baby's birth, you will follow instructions to put this sign on the door of your hospital room: QUIET PLEASE. INFANT STIMULATION IN PROGRESS.

How to Teach Your Baby to Read continues the tutoring that must continue to take place after baby is actually born. (Did you think you could slack off and just feed, change, and rock him?) Go out and buy some poster board and a felt-tipped marker, because flash cards will play heavily into the process.

Well aware that some "authorities" hotly dispute the value of infantile literacy, author Glenn Doman takes the offensive and says: Look, "tiny children" love to read. What else are they doing, crawling around and getting into everything and driving you and themselves crazy? Give them something they can put their intellectual milk-teeth into. Abstract symbols.

You may begin at three months if the child is exceptionally precocious. Otherwise, eight months to a year is fine. Just remember, says Doman, that after two years, the bloom is ever so slightly off the rose—and waiting until kindergarten, say, is a big mistake. (Doman ap-

provingly quotes an expert who told a mother whose child was illiter-
ate—unflash-carded—at age five: "Madame, run home quickly. You have
wasted the best five years of his life.")

Flash cards must be properly lettered. Doman says that the cards
must be six inches high and twenty-four inches long. The letters must
be five inches high, four inches wide, and about half an inch apart. Mar-
gins must be at least one-half-inch wide. Letters must be red. They must
be lowercase.

Words come next, in different sizes (progressively smaller) on dif-
ferent-sized flash cards (progressively smaller). Eventually, the letters will
be black. This progression must be followed exactly, "so that the child's
visual pathway may mature and gradually appreciate the material which
is being presented to his brain." I have my doubts about all this, but
Doman, who is the best-selling expert, asserts that his methods of enhancing intelligence have been well researched—among the brain-in-
jured.

Doman says that it is best to begin reading lessons with the words
"mommy," "daddy" and the child's name. Proceed to train as follows:

Find a quiet room in the house, without much furniture, pictures,
or "other objects which might distract the child's vision."

Hold up the flash card that says "mommy."

Tell him what it says.

Say no more. Whisk the card away.

Hold up the flash card that says "daddy."

Tell him what it says.

Say no more. Whisk the card away.

Do the same with three other words, but "do not ask your child
to repeat the words."

After the fifth word, "give your child a huge hug and kiss and
display your affection in the most obvious ways."

(Not including tearing up the flash cards and vowing to burn
them.)

Repeat three times a day.

Do this each day, adding new words, and praising your child: "[t]ell
your child that he is very good and very bright. Tell your child that you
are proud of him. Tell him that you love him very much."

Now, isn't that a telling sequence? If you're bright, kid, do stunts,
and make me proud, I'll love you—and this in the poor child's infancy!

Not surprisingly, Doman claims that children will learn to play this game "at lightning speed." Still, he cautions, do not do this more than three times a day, or "you will bore him." Do not show any card for more than a second, or "you will lose him." And do not test, at least not yet. Later, you can start picking up cards at random and asking him to read them to you. If he succeeds, why, tell him he is good and bright, you're proud of him, and love him, etc., etc. If not—well, "simply tell him enthusiastically what the word is—and go on."

"IT SAYS *MOMMY*, HONEY BUNCH!!!! CAN YOU SAY IT NOW??!?!"

Well, give it time.

In the meantime, do not neglect to develop your child's mathematical capacities, as illustrated in Doman's *How to Teach Your Baby Math*, because, as with reading, the critical period begins very early. In fact, Doman claims, numbers are best taught at one year of age or younger (it's never too early), and that, indeed, baby wants "desperately" to be taught such things.

Thus, he suggests that new mothers prepare flash cards, this time eleven by eleven inches. Mother will also need self-adhesive red dots, 5,005 of them, to be exact. These should be three-fourths-of-an inch in diameter. They will be placed on the flash cards. The first card will have one dot, the next, two, and so on, until baby learns to recognize—on sight—how many dots there are per card.

You can teach equations:

Put the "one," "two," and "three" cards on your lap.

"Using a happy and enthusiastic tone simply say, 'One plus two equals three.'"

Show the appropriate cards, to illustrate.

But practice first, says Doman. You don't want to be fumbling for your various dotted cards because "baby will simply creep away and he should. His time is valuable too."

After all, he could be learning what numerals look like. You could also show him numbers as high as "200," or "300"—Doman says your child will be thrilled. "After this come back and show him examples of 210, 325, 450, 586, 1830." He cautions, however: "Don't feel that you must show each and every numeral under the sun." Why? Doman confides that such excess might "bore" him.

Proof that you have started too late?

Doman suggests that you really should start at birth, since, after all, haven't you been "talking to him for the nine months prior to his delivery?" Baby must have been wondering where those flash cards were all along.

Now, for a newborn, your poster board alone should be fifteen by fifteen (you'll be a hit dragging this into the hospital). The dots have to be *"very* large," at least one-and-a-half inches in diameter. They should be black (like a black-and-white mobile). On day one, start with one dot, and say "one." You can do these each time you diaper your newborn. "This works very well," says Doman.

On day two, you can advance to two dots, but don't forget to train with the single-dotted card as well. Gradually increase your number of dots until you reach fourteen, confident in the knowledge that you have "actually grown [baby's] visual pathway." Baby will soon be ready for a "very fast-paced math program," and he has you to thank.

I'll just duck out of the way here.

Should you feel queasy on reading this chapter, you can thankfully cite the opinions of David Elkind and T. Berry Brazelton, among others, who believe that a trained toddler is a stress-twisted toddler. This is an example of how there are always two answers to the same question in the child-rearing business.

Experts come in handiest when bolstering one's own gut feeling. They are of great help in deflating, or at least balancing, the excesses of other experts. Parents tend to pick up the book that best suits their own biases. For instance, in one popular parents' magazine, one mother complains that you *have* to cram your child like a Loire Valley goose, or risk having him fall behind the others and suffer in preschool.

"Have a Genius" titles are going to appeal to one sort of parent; "Don't Rush the Poor Kid" titles are going to appeal to another.

Now if you were a kid, who would you pick to be your parent?

HINT: Parents who believe in unhurried childhoods and resist social pressure to turn their kids into status machines tend to bake more and better brownies.

NINETEEN

WHEREIN MOM NEEDS A NEWSLETTER TO CHART BABY'S PROGRESS

T he advertisement for *Growing Child* begins with a challenge that is, only slightly, also a threat:

CAN YOU ANSWER THESE 10 QUESTIONS ABOUT YOUR CHILD'S DEVELOPMENT?

Obviously, the question is rhetorical. Mom, Dad: Without the help of *Growing Child,* you cannot. Implicit is the prospect of doom, for you (ignoramus) and your luckless child. Subscribing to *Growing Child,* according to *Growing Child,* is "like having a good friend come to your home, a friend who's knowledgeable, comfortable and reassuring." It's also like having a friend who won't leave. *Growing Child* will come to your home, and come to your home, and keep on coming to your home every month (unless powerfully shown the door) until your child is—as they call it—"72 months"! In plain English, they are talking about advice-giving for the next six years.

And all because you couldn't answer those ten introductory questions:

Question One (in paraphrase): Why does a one-month old baby see only eight inches in front of him, and why should you turn this child from head to foot each day?

You should? Uh-oh.

Still, I'll attempt an *Answer:* My hunch on the distance thing is that if a newborn baby could see everything all at once, he'd explode. Better just to see Mom and Dad's face, rather than the crowds of the curious, the excess of play equipment, and the many, many catalogs that paper the house.

As for the head-to-foot maneuver, I *know* the answer. You move baby from head to foot every day because otherwise he'd be lying in his own spit-up. Baby spits up many times a day. You can move him *around* the head of the crib, but after a while, it's all wet. (Rate of spit-up exceeds rate of dry-up by a factor of ten.) Nor have you been clever enough to have laid in a supply of crib bibs, those neat little terries that tie to the crib (available by catalog). Nor do you launder three times a day. So after a while, as in the mad tea party, you simply move baby down the line to the cleanest part of the crib. He spits at the head, you move him to the foot, and vice versa on the morrow. Correct?

Wrong, and points deducted for frivolity. Spit-up has little to do with "your child's development," apart from the alimentary sense of the word.

Actually, I suspect that the right answer has something to do with that old Gymboree wisdom about stimulating both sides of the brain.

I never do find out the answer, because—slothful parent that I am—I do not whip out the checkbook until at least a month postpartum. My subscription (and indenture) to *Growing Child* does not begin until month three. Never mind. Because of my tendency to follow the "why not?" rubric, this ad has convinced me to spin my newborn, not only in the crib but on the changing table. I learn that I find both ends of him equally adorable (a Bonding Bonus!). As for the baby, he doesn't seem to mind discovering new perspectives on his eight inches of universe (by month three, perhaps it's nine or ten).

Question Two features a phenomenon called "face watching," and hones in on what faces a baby ought to watch.

My Answer: Here again, I feel I can venture the educated guess. Face watching, or "face watching," is basically the watching of faces, from the Latin word "face." Like, you have a face. I have a face. Our faces, however, are possibly different. Though each has two eyes, a nose, mouth, there are tiny variations that are infinitely interesting. Within the same face, moreover, are variations of lighting, mood, and time. We watch each other and are thus entertained through the dreariest of circumstances. You think, My, she looks tired—do I look as tired as she does? I think, Should I tell him about that smudge of shaving cream on his chin? And so on.

Baby does the same, and in doing so gains still another Bonding Bonus. Our faces are nature's imprintables for babies. They are programmed to stare at them, and are reinforced for doing so by their infinite variety and constant movement. Perhaps the fact that they are not true black-and-white is wasted on the child (this can be remedied by purchasing black-and-white faces to hang on the side of the crib, or in the convenient flash card form), but they are still mighty interesting. Almost as interesting as a $49.95 mobile, and less apt to grow monotonous, or fall on the child.

What about the second question, about which faces your baby really ought to watch?

Human ones, *Growing Child*. Particularly those of near relatives unscarred by humorlessness, or commercial grasping.

Wrong. After looking at the relevant issue (five months), I still can't answer the question, but what I can decipher has little to do with the human.

Here is what *Growing Child* tells me about the fine points of face watching:

In studies, it says, Baby is given two pictures to look at. Unseen researchers watch him, timing how long he stares at each picture. They determine which one he looks at longer. They determine that the one he looks at longer is the one he finds more interesting. They determine that babies like to look at faces that have eyes on top, nose in the middle, and mouth at the bottom, and that when offered the view of "a face having the eyes, nose and other features scrambled around into a meaningless mess, the baby [does] not give it much attention."

From all this we learn that babies have a "concept or idea" of what a face is. The newsletter helpfully adds that "a concept or idea is a kind of picture in his mind about what a thing is like."

By now, my concept or idea of *Growing Child* is slightly negative, owing to its ponderous obviousness. But there is more to learn, so I must keep reading my newsletter:

It tells me that baby has an image of Mother's face that is distinctive. When a new person comes along, it comes along with a slight variation on the theme of eyes, nose, mouth, and this, too, is interesting to baby.

"Is the new thing a face? Baby must study the pattern to make sure. He probably looks at the main landmarks . . . to see if they conform to the pattern that he has seen before." If eyes, nose, and mouth are generally in the right places, Baby will feel good about it. (If not, he won't; who would?) The smile Baby makes means that he is thinking: "I know what that is—it's a face."

Growing Child then tells us that "faceness" is a concept that was even "developed in your infancy . . ."

Even though Mom never got *Growing Child*.

". . . not through repetitious exposure to one face . . ."

Or theme.

. . . but from looking at lots of different faces.

Oh.

We are then told that baby will look around to see as many faces as possible, testing his concept of "faceness," noting small discrepancies, expanding his definition, learning, learning, learning, and even making new concepts when necessary, "or at least . . . subdivisions of the old."

"More about this in later months."

I am taking that last sentence as a threat, *GC*.

Question Three addresses your baby's babbling, and what your response to such babble should be.

    My Answer: A harsh "Shut up"?

    Just kidding, *Growing Child*.

I know. You know. We all know. You're supposed to respond to the babble. A good response is to imitate (a sincere form of flattery). Then wait. And he'll say something else. And then you'll say something, perhaps another echo. And so on. This will help Baby, as an adult, handle himself well on long, aimless telephone chats, or with a Freudian analyst.

Now skip to *Questions Five* and *Six*.

Question Five is scary. It asks what you could do, at five months, with the best intentions, that would have the inadvertent effect of delaying baby's ability to creep, "thus unfairly labeling the baby as 'slow.'"

Just between you and me, here is where things get ugly. Simple oversight. Delay. Labeling. "Slow." Do I hear threats here? Nonetheless, I know the answer. You must not tie your baby to the crib or leave him in the Kanga-Rocka-Roo or strapped into your Snugli. Rather, let baby move about a bit on the rug (vacuumed and mite-free), particularly on his tummy. Most important: Do not frequent places where baby is apt to be labeled in any way. Should he not begin to prop, lift, crawl, etc., in record time, enjoy the fact that you will not have to baby-proof in record time.

Question Six covers the crawling-into-a-corner-and-getting-stuck phenomenon (I hate it when that happens). What are you supposed to do about it? Why?

My Answer: Get him out of that corner and point him in the opposite direction? Why? Because (a) it is the kind thing and (b) it will stop the screams of rage and frustration?

Let's move on to the last question, which covers "unstructured play materials," what they are good for, and why some people don't like them.

My Answer: This one's easy. Unstructured play materials, unlike *Growing Child*, have no right or wrong answers. Dolls, crayons, balls, blocks, all can be played with in a variety of ways. (At least if you avoid certain Montessori schools.) Some parents dislike them because they do not lend themselves to testing, scores, and interviews by rigid school systems. Ambiguity creates anxiety, hence childhood—or more accurately, observing childhood—makes many adults anxious. To them I say: Squash some Play-Doh.

At this point, I have no idea how many questions I have answered correctly. But I am sure that I have erred in subscribing because my first letter from the company includes a quotation from Maria Montessori (author of a great multitude of structured play materials): "The most important period in life is not the age of university studies, but the period from birth to age six." The publisher adds: "By subscribing to *Growing Child*, you have indicated your agreement with this renowned educator."

By implication, my cancellation will indicate my agreement with a passel of rogues.

The publisher hopes that I will *not* cancel until my child's sixth birthday. He explains the issues involved: As it is, I will only be getting fifteen months of the newsletter. If I renewed every year until my child's sixth birthday, it would cost "$94.62 at today's subscription rate . . . and that rate could go up."

But if I renew from now *until* my child's sixth birthday, it will cost "only $80.37—"

So, in other words, put aside eighty dollars for five years, so that you can save less than fourteen dollars. Clearly, the man has never heard of bank interest. Still, he says, it's quite a bargain:

We are introduced to a brief lecture on the price of college, state or private (which can cost "$10,000, $15,000 or more per year!"). Now that our heads are reeling at the thought of our children at age eighteen (or, as *Growing Child* would put it, 216 months), we are ready for the hard sell: "The cost of $80.37," the publisher concludes, seems so little—it does, compared to Harvard—so "Please act now."

All *right*!

We are also made privy to a fan letter from a *Growing Child* subscriber, a veteran of six years:

> Dear Growing Child,
>
> I received my last issue . . . of growing child [sic] . . . what a tremendous help. . . . This was my first child, and believe me—I poured [sic] over all the baby books, child rearing books, etc. I was *so* nervous. But thank goodness for your monthly moments of calm. . . . From you, I learned not to pressure my son . . . to grow/

learn until he is ready. But yet, to discipline when things really count. I did not force my son to memorize numbers or letters, as many of my friends did. But Tommy could add + subtract long before his friends—why? Because I followed his signals—as you suggest—He liked to help me take coke [sic] cans apart when we buy them in 12-packs—from 4 yrs old, he *understood* the concept of $6+6=12$, $6-3+3$, $3+3+3+3=12$—not just memorizing numbers. *And* he had *FUN* learning it. . . .

Fun, for us, occurs more frequently on vacation.

TWENTY

FLEEING BABY, AND FLEEING WITH BABY

Ah, vacation: butt in the hammock, head in the clouds . . . surrender. Know something, Mom and Dad? You deserve it. Remember sloth and selfishness, before you had the little one? For a week or two, you're going to revisit it, and if something gets spilled on the floor, 'twon't be you picking it up. Wave for the waiter and order another one of those Zombies.

Hang on: What about the kid? Do you leave him behind and spend the whole vacation worrying, missing, feeling guiltily shackled, feeling guiltily unshackled? Or do you take him along and spend large parts of your vacation slathering baby SPF 40 and inveigling naps as your peers windsurf past you?

My friend Julie puts it succinctly: "With the kids along, it isn't exactly a vacation." (She's just had her third. Kid, not vacation.) "But if you go without them," she adds, "you miss 'em like crazy."

This may well be the paradox of parenthood.

First things first. You cannot think of leaving your child behind if you don't have someone reliable, whom your child knows and loves, to leave her with. Many people I know, people with romance in their hearts and foresight in their devious minds, have bragged about second honey-moons taken during the baby's first six months, with the grandparents playing Cupid. Fine. Just don't try that on a child much older than six months who hasn't seen extended family since birth. Flesh and blood mean nothing to a baby with stranger anxiety; if she doesn't know that face, she may not like that face, even though it's Grandma's and it's smiling.

(Now this is where you should have been reading your *Growing Child* and giving baby some practice with multivarious face formations, some with wrinkles and flour on the nose-bridge.)

In the case of a Grandma-shy baby, you are stuck—unless you have been wise enough and rich enough to have already engaged a regu-lar sitter, and that sitter is willing to live in full time during the week you're away.

You're starting to chicken out. You're starting to think that a week's too much. A day or two, that's the ticket. Yeah. A weekend at an inn, not too far away. A four-poster. A crackling fire.

But what if the house burns down? And what if the housekeeper is secretly a lonely, unfulfilled woman, a deluded wretch, no, an evil witch, who actually thinks the baby is hers, that you're the imposters? (Sometimes you think so, too.) Or what if—what if the baby forgets you entirely, forging a permanent bond with the person you have paid to help you? A person who will one day leave and break his heart!

Maybe you could get away for a couple of hours, you know, have a drink at the local bar or something. A drink with a paper parasol in it, of course. After which you could buy a glossy travel magazine and read it with your husband. In the bath, together, with Calgon? Like the owl and the pussycat?

Or maybe you could screw up your nerve—the one that made you take the plunge into crazy adventures like marriage and parent-hood—and go.

I thought I couldn't.

In my first child's sixth month, my husband and I planned a weeklong trip to the island of Grenada. Why did we choose a country best known as the site of American military intervention in 1983? A country that, if you won a date on some game show, the announcement "all-expenses-paid trip to Grenada!" would probably make your face fall? We chose it because our then-baby-sitter, the famous Queenie, was

Grenadian. Like some latter-day Victorian, I thought I could have my lover, the nanny, and the child, accompany me to my island in the sun. Trade winds would blow, lovers would love, Nanny would mind the child—and the child? The child would frolic, naked, toes tickled by the warm, caressing waves. At night we'd all eat papaya, slobbering like pigs, and laughing, laughing.

Queenie was happy to go along. She hadn't seen her ninety-eight-year-old grandmother in years, she told us. The woman to whom she felt closest in the world.

There is an oft-repeated tenet about travel with children: Something unexpected always happens. The child won't sleep, the child won't eat, the child gets a rash. In our case, something more major happened. A day before we were supposed to leave, Queenie's grandmother died.

Now Queenie (who feared funerals) was not going to go to Grenada, and neither was our child. Taking her along sans Queenie would have meant nonstop shlep and toil, more work and worry than staying at home.

My husband sported a subtle gleam at the prospect of leaving our Victorian entourage behind. Queenie, who worked for us part-time, volunteered to stay with Emma, no problem. And my parents, who have seen the child every weekend since birth, offered to check in periodically, to put out fires, halt burglaries, that sort of thing.

It was the first time I had ever left Emma for more than a few hours. And I took a plane. In my emotional vocabulary, that meant that I risked orphaning my child. At moments during the flight, I morbidly pondered which would be worse for her: losing her mother and father in a plane crash, or dying with her mother and father in a plane crash? For my part, I was glad that she would remain free of the crash. You can see what a romantic and hot getaway partner I was already becoming.

We got to Grenada alive, and I started looking around me.

When you leave a child behind, you see them everywhere. Our hotel was full of them. Children. Newborns in wicker baskets, toddlers in jungle bikinis, water splashing from their clumsily carried pails. Fly-netting over pudgy pink cheeks. Peals of laughter at the water's edge. Hahahaha.

Our child was in freezing New York City, with a grieving Grenadian and no mother or father (who still might crash on the flight home).

We called home that night.

"How is she? How is she?"

"Who? Oh, Emma, she's *terrific!* She's standing up right now."

Whazzat? Standing? She had never stood up before. She had never stood up for us. She had never stood up, period.

"Are you sure?"

"Oh, yeah." Laughter. "Emma, you hang on now."

"What's she hanging on to?"

"The crib bar. She's lookin' at me talkin.'"

Oh. Our child had stood up out of a superhuman effort to get to the phone. That made sense.

We called the next night.

"Emma got two teeth now," said Queenie.

When we had left, our Emma had been toothless.

"What? Teeth? Are you sure?"

"Sure! Show Queenie your teeth, honey! She showin' me her teeth now."

"Oh. They must be cute, huh?"

On the third night, Queenie said, "You know, I think she said 'Mama' today."

"Really?" I was excited. She missed me, her own true mama.

"Yeah, I think so. I was feedin' her, and she looked at me, in the eye and said 'Mama.'"

Looked at *you,* did she?

"Could have been 'Mmm-mmm,' though," Queenie amended, thus perhaps saving her job. "Like, enjoyin' her food."

"But I *think* it was 'Mama,'" Queenie continued, thus perhaps forfeiting her job. "She said it pretty, and she said it pretty clear."

"We will talk later, Queenie." When I regain the clarity of my own diction, I thought.

I took to the four-poster with a copy of *The First Twelve Months of Life,* one of the many essentials of child-rearing that are loaded with unhappy and unwanted information. (My favorite, though, is Burton White's *The First Three Years of Life,* not only because it extends the informational agony from one year to three, but for its fierce admonition—that I also ignored—that children spaced less than three years apart may be permanently damaged, and eternally at strife.)

I was reading a child-care book as a substitute for having my child with me. It was, of course, a poor substitute, more Dear John than billet-doux. In no time at all, I found this jolly TNT:

"This prewalking period is no time for any unnecessary separation from you. . . ."

Call in the defense to define "necessary," please.

> [Some of the] finest research to date on the nature of parent and child attachment says "The protest, despair and detachment that typically occur when a child over six months is separated from his mother are due to loss of maternal care at this highly dependent, highly vulnerable stage of development. The child's hunger for his mother's presence is as great as his hunger for food, and her absence generates a powerful sense of loss and anger."
>
> . . . the trauma of early loss or separation from the mother can carry over to produce similar responses in older individuals. Such disturbed adults tend to make excessive demands upon others. . . .

Powerful. Loss. Anger. *Disturbed adulthood.*

In other words, don't go anywhere, and if you do, you will pay. Forever.

And note no mention of the father, the grandparents, or that hand-picked baby-sitter who has been eliciting all those chuckles. This is why I love those helpful books. By the way, do those disturbed adults' "excessive demands upon others" include the demand that they never take a breather until the child is (largely) through with separation issues?

I'd like another Zombie now, waiter.

And I'll tell you how it worked out for us. We flew home shortly after. We had to stop over unexpectedly in Trinidad. There was an epidemic of yellow fever in Trinidad. Had Emma come with us, she would have been exposed to a deadly disease. As it was, we had merely ruined her mentally and emotionally.

We got home. It was way past Emma's bedtime. We did not expect to see her until morning.

We walked through the door and saw Queenie.

At the sound of our voices Emma shot up in her crib. She stood, screaming "Dada! Baba! Mama!" (showing both of those teeth), and hugged me, hugged him, and beamed.

TWENTY-ONE

HOMEMADE HELP

Wistful for any escape short of travel, dying for a change of perspective and the occasional pat on the shoulder from someone who knew me before the Change of Life, I think about my children's two sets of grandparents. Though this topic, like so many before it, is a contemporary bandwagon, with "clubs" for elders to join, books to read on "how to grandparent," and "experts" ready to advise on strengthening the intergenerational bonding process, it's hard to scoff it off.

There *is* a need for rapprochement within families, particularly those for whom the question of advice-giving has always been a touchy one. Emancipated from their heavy childhood home, some new parents simply do not want to re-experience it, even through the glistening eyes of their children. In turning away from their past, they may be losing the occasional wise nugget, loads of baby-sitting hours, and a bit of independence from outside advisers whose main motive is the dollar.

Once upon a time, and a very nice time it was, grandmothers sported white buns and smelled gingery, grandfathers wore cardigans and whittled things, and muddy-shoed grandkids came calling all the time. Nowadays, more likely than not, children see their grandparents twice a year in passionate, hectic bursts—or not at all. Ours is an age of busy nomadism, of splintered families, fuzzy traditions, and a changing picture of "old" folks. Married children (who have often spent college at least a time zone away) don't necessarily re-root near the family homestead—if there is a homestead. Should they end up divorcing, more moves become possible. One set of grandparents may no longer fit into the scene—indeed, may be edged off it by fuming exes and/or the arrival of brand-new children (and brand-new grandparents). And even in the most stable families, grandparents themselves may have other things to do (cruises, courses, third careers) than pinch-hit for Mom and Dad whenever the need arises.

My own family is a cross-section of modern grandparenthood, with the paternal grandparents tucked remotely in a small English village, and the maternal a companionate ten-minute drive away. Both sets seem as involved as it is possible to be. Our children experience their English grandmother primarily through long, loving cards filled with doting questions and descriptions bordering on the Shelleyan. Neither can yet read these cards nor understand the yearning passions with which every margin is crammed, but they do appreciate the adorning pictures (ducks in waistcoats, kitties in bloomers, milkmaids in bonnets), and I suspect that they will treasure the contents, too, when they become more literate.

Emma and Gabriel's experience of their New York grandparents comes in the form of a weekly Sunday visit. My folks are the sort who *really* baby-sit (which involves less sitting and more chasing around the house, tossing in the air, and proffering cookies), while my husband and I gratefully gallivant. We pretend to have retired; they pretend to be new parents. It's a good deal all around.

For those of us lucky enough to have a grandparent somewhere—anywhere—in the picture, they can provide a vital part of family life. "Children who know their grandparents are very different from those who don't," says Dr. Arthur Kornhaber, a psychiatrist from Lake Placid, New York, whose intergenerational studies are documented in the book *Grandparents, Grandchildren: The Vital Connection* (co-written with Kenneth Woodward). "They have a special emotional sanctuary. They feel secure; they know they belong to a group of people." (According to his studies, children without such close ties express their deprivation by drawing their grandparents as impersonal stick figures.) Fostering this bond, regardless of geographical or emotional distance between grandparents and their children, should therefore be a priority. Of all the gifts one can give a child—most of ours have rooms stuffed with goodies—this familial closeness will be the most long-lasting.

Indeed, according to Dr. Harold Bloomfield, a psychiatrist in Del Mar, California, and author of *Making Peace with Your Parents,* grandparents are more important now than ever: "They provide that sense of continuity," he says, stressing that so much today—from coffee cups to the latest toy to family itself—is throwaway. Dr. Bloomfield feels that children benefit greatly from understanding that their family has deep roots, stretching over time and place. "My own mother is an immigrant from Germany," he says. "This gives my daughter a sense of cultural differences, of the ups and downs of life from place to place and over the years. Her sense of the past and of her own identity is enriched." At eighty-four, Dr. Bloomfield's mother also gives her granddaughter "a sense of the life cycle; what it means to age." Dr. Arthur Kornhaber has actually found that children who have little or no contact with their grandparents may be more prejudicial toward, or more frightened by, aspects of aging than those who retain close bonds to their elders.

One fourteen-year-old, alienated from her grandmother by her parents' divorce, disclosed, sobbingly, that she now "hated" old people, and wanted to "kick them in their wrinkled faces." Perhaps even worse, she dreaded her own aging process: "When I see old people hobbling along I think I'll commit suicide before I become like that." While that girl's reaction is, of course, extreme, Dr. Kornhaber feels that such negativity prevails when children and their elders are kept at an uncomfortable distance. Dr. Matti Gershenfeld, adjunct professor of Psychoeducational Processes at Temple University in Philadelphia and a family therapist, adds, "If the child never spends much time with his grandparents, he'll be more aware of their wrinkles or disabilities, and may not want to see them. The generational gap," she concludes, "may be harder to bridge."

Since the fastest-growing segment of the American population is those aged seventy or older, this gap—if it continues to exist—will become more and more apparent. Luckily, says Dr. Kornhaber, more and more grandparents are assuming what he calls a "heroic" stance: "By asserting themselves as Great Parents they challenge a system of age relations which patronizes the aged and conspicuously denies any real value to the grandparent-grandchild relationship."

More heroic still are the children who understand what their elders are for. Dr. Kornhaber cites the opinion of a six-year-old boy on the subject of an ailing grandmother to whom he has been close: "Grandma's *body* is getting smaller, but Grandma is not shrinking. Just her body."

The greatest side effect of grandparenting is indisputably a sweet one. Love, love, love, say all the experts: There is *nothing* like the kind that skips a generation. "Mother may say, 'You are lazy or no good at math.' But Grandma will say, 'You are funny, you are cute, you are great to have around.'" says Dr. Gershenfeld. According to her, many an adult remembers getting through a tough childhood simply because one grandparent believed in him unconditionally and vice versa. ("I constantly hear, 'My grandfather was such a great man, I decided to model myself on him,'" she says.) "It's a deep, deep feeling," agrees Dr. Bloomfield. "A unique love system," agrees Dr. Kornhaber, "that only nature could create."

What's unique about it may have a lot to do with the enriching perspective of age, something rarely appreciated in our time. Child-development expert Dr. David Elkind has long noticed an overly ambitious streak to modern parenthood. Exemplified by flash cards, cram courses, and aerobics for neonates, this trend has caused some children to be prodded, at earlier and earlier ages, toward greater and greater "achievements." This feather-in-my-cap agenda, Dr. Elkind feels, is far less important to grandparents. What *they* care about, bless them, is the child himself. Having "made their mark," they are able, more often than parents, to relax and "appreciate the child without excessive ego involvement." They are the ones who remind us that Johnny would be happier hitting a ball than balancing on a beam (or sawing that viola); they are the ones who do *not* think Jenny's small-motor activity is lagging behind her (ten-month-old) peers'. They are wise enough to treasure, and enjoy, each child for who he or she is.

Not surprisingly, there are just as many types of grandparents, and grandparenting styles, as there are children. Dr. Kornhaber still believes the ideal to be the closely connected grandparent, who might live in the same house as the grandchildren or see them almost daily. Only about 15 percent of modern grandparents retain such ties to their grandchildren, according to the psychiatrist, who decries the modern trend of older folks flying South for their winter years, disengaging from the families who still need them—whether they know it or not. Dr. Kornhaber's extensive interviews with grandparents and grandchildren indicate, he claims, that both suffer lifelong grief—typically suppressed—when this intense connection is lost.

Since most grandparents *do* live more than a stone's throw away, it is reassuring to know that most experts don't urge them to pick up and move into the spare room. Assuming that such a scenario would please most parents, which it wouldn't, it would tend to unsettle (if not deeply irritate) many modern grandparents, who increasingly have busy lives of their own.

As sociologists Andrew J. Cherlin and Frank F. Furstenberg, Jr., authors of *The New American Grandparent*, point out, "How many older people who have worked hard all their lives could be dissuaded from retiring to a condominium in the Sunbelt?" Nor do they feel that parents—caught between two ostensibly love-starved generations—should suddenly quit their jobs and rent a U-Haul to be near the mythical hearth. Both generations, they feel, are entitled to a bit of psychological space, if they need it.

"I've done my job," says the paternal grandmother of three-year-old Aubrey and six-month-old Meg. "No more Diaperland for me, thank you." When Karin, a full-time mother whose "Diaperland" is in New York, is visited by this grandmother (who lives in Ohio), she must remember that small children are not universally pleasing to some, who may remember the draining drudgery of early motherhood with something of a shudder. It's small comfort for Karin to know that this hands-off policy might subside when the kids learn not to slurp out of the soup bowl—or fling it at the wall. "What she has to realize is that some grandparents are not going to want to be automatic baby-sitters, and it's their prerogative," says Dr. Bloomfield. "You have to be sensitive to who your parents are. Some can't take the day-to-day physical and psychological stresses anymore—but they can still be loving grandparents if you let them."

Sebastian, the four-year-old son of my Japanese friend Akiko, has even greater problems with his recently widowed American grandmother. "Oh, he *hates* her," says Akiko, a part-time schoolteacher. "Even when he was a newborn, she didn't show him much attention." Why not? "He was the first grandson," she speculates. "His grandfather loved him more than he had *ever* loved anyone else. So maybe she was jealous."

Possibly, too, it's a matter of temperament. This same grandmother dotes on Sebastian's well-mannered seven-year-old sister: "She calls Danica a 'good' child, but says Sebastian is 'plain mischief.' She doesn't like the noise and mess that he makes." When such favoritism is "not a figment of the parent's imagination," says Dr. Gershenfeld, it's helpful to make the grandparents aware that they may be hurting the less-favored child and to suggest ways to bring out the best in each individual. For instance, if Johnny is too young and restless for restaurants (and Jenny isn't), maybe it would be good to plan a special park outing for Johnny—where his tendency to dribble ice cream down his neck doesn't matter so much.

For those of us with substantial gaps dividing generations, it is reassuring to know that they are far from unbridgeable. Recognizing the need for greater "grandparenting consciousness," Dr. Kornhaber started the Foundation for Grandparents nine years ago. Now, he says proudly, there are nationwide Grandparents' Days in schools, laws in all fifty states to protect grandparents' visitation rights, and even "expectant grandparents" programs in hospitals. It really is the hot new issue in child-rearing. (Headed by experts as usual.)

The secret to long-distance grandparenting may indeed lie in early bonding. "It helps that they have seen that little baby unfold, that they've seen the stages of early development, and have had the opportunity to be excited about the wonders of that child," according to Dr. Gershenfeld. Grandparents who have seen a child from the earliest days, weeks, or months seem irrevocably touched by the most unreasonable kind of love—the kind you need when, a little later, your vases are toppled off their tables and your draperies pulled to the floor. "They've gone through the stage of being loved unconditionally by that child." The good feelings are mutual: "When you hold a baby, he likes it, and he identifies you with that good feeling." It's harder to establish that elemental love later, says Dr. Gershenfeld, when kids start becoming "differentiated, seeing things differently." Those who have made the early connection, however, will say, "Yes, I like Grandma, even if her hearing's bad, or she's a little strange. She's part of my family."

After this initial process, mutual visits, rare as they may be, can go a long way. (In order to facilitate this contact, the Foundation for Grandparents has originated a Grandparent/Grandchild Camp in New York's Adirondack Mountains.) Dr. Bloomfield, for example, says that if you can manage one time a year—however brief—that grandchild and grandparent can spend some time together, you've built something good and lasting. That time, however, must be orchestrated with flexibility and sensitivity to the needs and limitations of all three generations. Recognize that there may be an initial awkwardness, that some visits will have to be as brief as a couple of days, and that children—especially during longer visits—will not spend every waking moment having in-depth conversations about life in the forties. "Take them someplace really nice, without the parents, and spend some money on them," suggests Dr. Gershenfeld, who also provides an inexpensive little gift for her grandchildren when she greets them at the airport. "They should know they're in for good times when they see you," she advises. "Create an adventure."

Brave Dr. Bloomfield was about to embark on a cruise in which his typically lively seven-year-old would share a cabin with her typically not-so-lively octogenarian grandmother. "We decided on ten days, not two weeks," he says, "since my mother has pointed out to me that she's not fifty-three anymore." And, if within those ten days, the little girl proves "too much" for her doting but not superhuman grandmother, she'll switch over to her parents' cabin. "With these matters, it's often a stamina question, and you have to be sensitive," says Dr. Bloomfield.

Dr. Gershenfeld, too, is all in favor of at least one annual visit for long-distance grandparents, bridged from year to year by letters. (Her correspondence includes pictures taken of herself and the grandchildren from previous visits.) Until the age of about ten, she feels, children are not the hottest telephone conversationalists. (They tend to nod a lot, mouth-breathe, and pass the phone, clattering, to someone else.) "But they *love* to get mail," she says. (As do their parents!) "It makes them feel really special. Send them interesting post-cards and stickers to collect, and really keep aware of what's going on in their lives. If you're not a part of somebody's life, there's nothing to tell. You'll ask how they are, what's new. You'll get nothing. But if you keep in touch, there's always a lot to tell."

Both Akiko's children, for example, are close with their Japanese grandparents, whom they see for an extended visit once a year, either here or across the Pacific. "Even before Danica could write, she'd send drawings to Japan, and I'd read her grandmother's letters." Akiko took great pains, she says, to teach her children Japanese phrases and customs, so that the different generations could understand each other. She also recognizes the importance of having Danica and Sebastian visit her ancestral home on a regular basis. This year, the children will celebrate their summer birthdays in Japan. "My mother gives them special food, plays with them, and makes them feel important. To them, she's the best friend in the world," says Akiko, describing what may be the core of modern grandparenthood.

According to Cherlin and Furstenberg, this friendly, "companionate" style is predominant today in a way unknown at the turn of the century, where grandparents (ginger smells and wood-whittling notwithstanding) tended to command some real authority. Now, more often than not, grandparents are perceived as their grandkids' buddies, allies, confidantes. They are there, in a sense, to buffer the effects of parenthood, offering an ear, a hug, and perspective.

Though they tend not to interfere directly with their children's roles as parents—going along with the modern trend to give grown children full autonomy and space—certain frictions inevitably occur. "Values are going to collide," says Dr. Gershenfeld. "Some grandparents are shocked by how the rules have changed, how casually some children dress on special occasions, for instance—jeans and sneakers instead of suits and dresses."

Modern-day lenience might also offend some elders. Grandma might say, "Shouldn't he be potty-trained by now?," and Grandpa might say, "You let them watch TV before breakfast?" Since many grandparents become totally besotted by their grandchildren—in a way they may not have been as parents—the reverse, too, is likely to happen. "Grandparents are frequently exploited and manipulated," says Dr. Elkind—and they seem to enjoy it. So Mom will say, "You gave her bubblegum before supper?" And Dad will say, "You gave ten dollars to a six-year-old?"

Experts (who are, naturally, big on value imposition themselves) tend in this case to counsel a good bit of breeziness. These family clashes, they say, are inevitable, and usually around the grandparental "vices" of sweets and spoiling. So, they say, Big Deal.

"The truth is, your child is not going to be damaged because one or the other grandparent does something differently than you," says Dr. Bloomfield. In fact, he adds, "It's good for them to know that for different people there are different agendas." ("It's like learning different customs for different countries," says Dr. Elkind.) In any case, parents should not fly off the handle—"Try to observe, not always react," he says. "You're not going to change them anyway," says Dr. Bloomfield, who urges parents to make their points, if they must, calmly—and out of the childrens' earshot.

Dr. Gershenfeld offers an even better reason for not flipping out: "Your children model after your behavior. If you relate to your parents badly, they'll relate to you badly. So don't be defensive, and don't try to control your parents. Your kids should see, by your actions, that, yes, sometimes parents can be difficult, relationships get sticky—but you still deal with them, and you still love them."

"It's worth a little hassle on the parents' side so that kids can have those good times with their grandparents," says Dr. Bloomfield. Beyond the "good times," of course, lies a critical foundation for the child's emotional—perhaps even spiritual—development, his sense that life is full, deep, and varied.

Building family bridges may be irksome at times, leading to fantasies of returning to Grenada sans impediment, forever. But the benefits to those we love—our parents *and* our children—seem worth it. What could be cozier than being sandwiched between two generations that for mystical reasons adore each other? And even if parents tend to treat their grandchildren like what Dr. Kornhaber terms "cronies against the common enemy," again: Big Deal. That's their role, their pleasure, and their privilege. And someday—if we're lucky—it'll be ours.

TWENTY-TWO

REMEDIAL CLASSES FOR PARENTS

Most of us are not all that close, physically or emotionally, to our immediate family. Grandparents do not live around the corner. Or if they do, we wish they'd move. Or they have, to those famous warmer climes. So parenthood's a bafflement, a new thing; as far as we know, we're the first ones ever to have done it. And everything else that we've ever done went so well! It all went perfectly. So why do we feel so dumb in the face of our screaming tyke, our colicky newborn, our bratty nine-year-old, of whom we are sometimes scared?

We parents should learn one thing in the modern era. We should accept that we need help, professional help. The sort that tells you that everything you do leads to years on the couch (so why not hop on now?). The sort that tells you how to discipline with love, love with discipline, and how to do it all with the background smell (real or ersatz) of good pies baking.

It will take money, time, and three-ring binders. You will need to consult many experts and take many courses and sharpen many Number 2 pencils. The modern gate to peace of mind is strait, unsure, and pricey.

The modern world can scare you anytime. It can start with a six-year-old's rudeness to the housekeeper, or a teenager's smirk at a home-less woman's socks. It can start with a daughter who wants to be "hot" or a son who wants to be "cool." It can start with the sight of a four-year-old taunting a friend or an eight-year-old glued to the soaps.

Indeed, for some parents, the fretting begins before the kid crawls. Is he overly greedy for those blocks? Why does he want more than two—hasn't he got only two hands? Is he going to be the next Ivan Boesky (without the jailhouse Bible classes)? Will he grow up smug, un-happy, a bigot?

All these niggling worries can make a parent wonder what and who he's feeding, spiritually. And when anxiety grows, modern parents do something about it: They go looking for help, wherever, and whenever, they can find it.

"At ten-twenty I dash out, and I'm back at my desk by ten after twelve," a television-network executive confides, describing the schedul-ing of her parenting group each Tuesday. There, she meets her two-and-a-half-year-old son (delivered by his nanny), eleven nonworking mothers, and a "parent facilitator." "Being busy doesn't mean you're less concerned about your child's development," the woman explains. "Any residual guilt I have about being away all day is dealt with. And for my son, who lives in this crazy world without real community, it's a time to socialize."

For the parents, particularly the working ones, a workshop is a chance to be with or talk about their kids. For mothers at home, a semi-nar is one of the best outings on the never-ending mashed-banana circuit. And for those with troublesome children—or children at troublesome ages (toddlers, teens), a lecture forum is one place to start getting help.

Guidance does not come cheaply. "You have to be upscale to even think of going," says a single mother, the director of a nonprofit institute. "Most mothers in my group don't bring their children," meaning they have hired help. "Even the ones who don't work"—and these are in the majority—"have home care, so they can do other things for themselves. And the sessions themselves are expensive."

Indeed, with the average two-hour class costing about twenty-five dollars, morality gurus in big cities like New York gross about a quarter of a million dollars a year. And that's just for the seminars.

Late in the eighties, a mother in an affluent New Jersey suburb placed an urgent phone call to Michael Schulman, a child psychologist. She told him that she had read and admired his book, *Bringing Up a*

Moral Child, which he had written with his wife, Eva Mekler. She told him that she had heard of his work in another suburb, where parents (coached by Schulman) had pressured reluctant school officials to introduce ethical issues into the curriculum. She told him she believed that the kids in her own white-collar community were growing up without consciences.

Schulman was interested and sympathetic. Just as the community began to arrange for his visit, a group of local high school jocks sexually assaulted, in the basement of one of their homes, a retarded girl they all knew.

Some of their classmates said the boys, all popular, had talked freely about the episode, even laughing about it. Others said they had heard of plans to repeat it, this time with the aid of a videotape camera. The papers caught every nuance of this apparent sociopathy in the middle class.

Shamed by its sudden notoriety, the town broke off contact with Schulman. "They pulled their wagons around," he said, with the patient, unflappable manner of his profession. "It took a while before they realized that they still needed to see me."

The next call, this time initiated by the local superintendent of schools, came that summer. What emerged over time was an eighteen-session package of "character education," as Schulman called it, geared toward different age groups, including the parents themselves, who would be asked to carefully follow the program. *Bringing Up a Moral Child* became the curricular spine, the new secular Bible.

But while hundreds of parents swarmed into Schulman's seminars (which, in their philosophical explorations, seemed more Socratic than Falwellian), some teachers remained wary.

"They were afraid of having schools get into moral education again," Schulman said, acknowledging an earlier time when the Seven Deadly Sins were part of every syllabus. "People nowadays are wary of being thought too nice; they connect it to weakness. I try to convince them that there's no way *not* to communicate a moral view. If you walk away from an issue, that's one view. If you take a stand, that's simply another. Both are messages that set up moral criteria."

In the end, Schulman adopted the term "character" education rather than "moral" education, because "'moral,'" he sighs, "is a hot word at the moment, with connotations of zealotry."

Too true: What the *M*-word connotes to disdainful babyboomers is not just zealotry but repression. Prayer in class, Anita Bryant, and Creationism come to mind, all anathema to those of us who grew up under the playful, drowsy eye of Dr. Spock. (It's hard to believe that any of our contemporary multibillionaires got where they are simply by remembering to say "after you.")

Now comes parenthood, shuffling the deck and ruffling the psyche. Most of us former pot heads are worried that while we know all there is to know about life, the universe, and ourselves, we don't know nothin' 'bout raisin' babies. (We're not completely "raised" ourselves.)

Scores of books join Schulman's in reflecting a growing parental confusion, books like *Raising Your Child to Be a Mensch, Raise Your Kids Right,* and *Positive Discipline.* The homespun tomes of T. Berry Brazelton and Penelope Leach (dealing mostly with milk, bath, and bowel) share shelf-space with the more alarmist *Raising PG Children in an X-Rated World, Who's in Control?,* and *High Risk: Children Without Conscience.* Huge stacks of books on beating your child into Christian submission loom in the chain-store bookshop. A typical example notes the comparison between child and savage, child and dog (also made to be beaten), child and devil. Scary stuff, and selling quite briskly.

Middle-class parents have long become used to yammering headlines about drug-addicted, alcohol-soaked thirteen-year-olds. Those "bad" kids have always been up to something sordid—in someone else's backyard. What they're not so used to are headlines about their own patch of manicured lawn, and—worse—the evidence before their eyes. Where "good" teens once shocked their parents by threatening to live off the land, on a houseboat, or in Kenya, today's breed is more likely to obsess about big bucks, cool wheels, and hot dates: using and getting.

Privileged or not, parents are starting to face problems not so very different from those of the inner city. The brunt of Schulman's work in a group home setting in the Bronx, for instance, is to translate teen status into human terms: "You remind the kids of the good feelings they've had giving and receiving love, as opposed to just watching TV, using people, taking drugs, or spending money." Only now are bourgeois parents beginning to realize the short moral step from the South Bronx to Westchester, from the slums to the suburbs.

For rich families as well as poor, attitudes toward getting and spending are passed on from generation to generation. Here is a recent (pre-holiday) scene at a parenting class on the chic East Side of Manhattan, one of hundreds of classes taking place all over town: Sandra Mann, a family therapist and doctor of child development, presides. The room is filled with well-groomed women, all in their thirties, all—but for the toddlers clinging to their knees and wrinkling their chenille blouses—resembling the high-income professionals they used to be. Now, instead of studying spreadsheets, they fret the minutiae of motherhood. They go to seminars and intensive workshops like this topping them off with the odd evening lecture at the Y. Sitting in class, they search the kind, wise face of the group leader who for a year (sometimes more) will supervise the way they act as parents.

For the moment Mann is *their* mother, the idealized one who does everything right. She is their mentor, their guru. When they graduate, they will ace motherhood, they hope. Their kids will not be in jail, or even on the couch. Where will they be? Harvard. "We're trying to discourage that fast-track mentality," says pleasant white-haired Mary Solow, director of the program. "But for some parents, all they can think about is going from the Parenting Center to this school's nursery"—which is prestigious—"and on to the Ivy League. Sometimes we have to show them that that's not what makes for happiness," she says.

"What kind of people do you want your kids to be?" asks Mann, friendly and folksy behind her large glasses. The question silences the buzzing room. Mann and the mothers have been talking about Christmas, Hanukkah, Manhattan preschoolers, and greed.

Greed may be good to Gordon Gekko, but it is anathema to Mann. Like Schulman, she is a "facilitator" with more than bed-wetting on her mind. One parent worries about her daughter watching money "fly" out of cash machines. Mann, smiling, notes, "Yes, there's a message." Suddenly, all the parents are asking about what to do about demands for this gift and that. (Catalogs have made life hell for some parents.) One mother says, "I came up with 'tomorrow.' Whenever he asks 'Can I have this?' I say 'Tomorrow.'"

"What are you going to say when he's ten years old?" asks Mann. "Will you have rules by then?" The room is again quiet. "And where will they come from?" One woman says, defiantly, that she had been deprived of toys as a child, that she (like everyone else in the room) could afford most toys, and that she intended to buy them.

Mann pauses, as though expecting a barrage of protest from everyone else in the room. There is none. Finally, she says, "It's easy to give your child everything. Easy. Give him a good VCR and a bunch of tapes and he won't bother you all day, right?" Everyone laughs. "So why not do it?" After a pause, she says, "What kind of adult are you forming—a happy, self-sufficient one, or one who's never satisfied?" Again, silence.

"It's getting harder and harder for children to delay gratification," says Mann. "You press a button, money comes out; they ask for something, you run and get it." One mother interjected, "This connects to drinking and drugs, right?" Mann: "Right. How are they going to deal with life? With frustration? With boredom? It's a whole new issue for our generation. Parents have the means to say yes all the time. But what are the consequences—the long-term consequences—of not saying no?"

Some "experts" are not so worried by modern parents' ethical dilemmas (and buying frenzies). Publishers, particularly, happily step into the bottomless well of parental generosity and fear. There is *The Don't Abuse Your Body Book,* a particular boon to the busy parent, says Grace Freedson, managing editor of Barron's. "Kids are often alone, and at younger and younger ages they are becoming aware of the lure of drugs, smoking, and drinking. It makes a wonderful, practical gift."

With a series of depressing drawings (featuring pallid abusers, steadily growing greener), the book explains addiction in terms a ten-year-old will understand. Along the same fin-de-siècle lines is the recently released *What to Do When You're on Your Own,* an exhaustive (and frightening) handbook that covers everything from not telling fibs to giving yourself the Heimlich. Bible books are published in board form; toddlers can now experience the expulsion from Eden without needing an adult to turn the page.

Most prevalent on the scene, however, is a growing list of mailbox-stuffing entrepreneurs, promising to solve ethical puzzles without parental intervention, reading, or attendance in workshops and seminars. These mail-order companies tend to make similar pitches: They reassure busy parents that their kids *will* be responsible, caring, and kind—if they read the books. One typical series, "Learn the Value of," sells a vast sequence of titles with themes like "Courage," "Faith," "Love," "Fairness," and even "Humor" and "Joy."

This company puts its firm finger on our fluttery moral pulse: "You, as parents, want your children to have values to guide them through difficult times and through times of temptation. You want your children to be equipped to make the right decisions. You want them to know *the right things to do.* . . . But—

"—most values have to be acquired, usually learned through example . . . sometimes through painful experience."

Acquired? Learned through example? Painful experience? If these seem harsh alternatives, the entrepreneurs offer an easier path:

"But *now, with this new series* [my italics], 'Learn The Value Of. . . ,' your children can *teach themselves* the very values you want them to learn. . . ."

In other words, you can just sign up and close the door on your child, quietly lisping his lessons in the book-lined den. When he emerges, bleary-eyed (having read all twenty-eight volumes), but radiant with the joy of moral wisdom, you'll have (own?) a do-gooder, even-tempered, untemptable—or your money back.

Another company, the "Living Skills Press," offers cartoonish books "designed to teach personal, social and coping skills." After reading the material, children will definitely "assume responsibility for personal obligations," "make good decisions," "find positive ways to correct [their] own misbehavior." Imagine how much leisure time this could free up for the busy parent.

It's easy to question the (commercially wishful) proposition that lapses in parenting can be covered by the book of the month. Barbara Ehrenreich, the social commentator and author of *Fear of Falling: The Inner Life of the Middle Class*, says, "It's a little silly to think of values as something you inject, instead of live. It reminds me of this idea they had a few years ago of teaching ethics to medical students—you worried that they'd probably cheat on the ethics exams." But even Ehrenreich adds, "It may be better than nothing." Meaning: If you can't say no to Junior, throw one of these books into his grab bag and hope for a miracle.

Nancy Samalin, virtually a household name on the parenting circuit, is all too familiar with insatiable kids and their hesitant parents. Disparaging these books tailored to children ("God, they're boring!"), she herself is author of the widely read *Loving Your Child Is Not Enough* (a handbook on modern discipline). In addition, Samalin runs workshops, seminars, and lectures everywhere in town, from Bank Street to Lenox Hill to her own Upper West Side apartment. Some mothers (and a handful of fathers) have been going to her "groups" for years, *years;* it's like therapy—and no children allowed.

Samalin sits in her living room, a palatial salon of chinoiserie, shells, and odd anthropological artifacts. You might well be in the ante-room of a grand old shrink, one with a goatee and a Viennese accent. The workshop over, the parental din fades, and the grand gray Hudson floats by, just behind Samalin's calm back.

Tall and well-heeled, soignée and slightly prim, she analyzes the modern parent. "They're stuck in the 'happiness trip.' It's such a contemporary phenomenon," she says, crossing her long legs. "The ones that are working come home and want 'quality time.' They *don't* want to have their brief conversation with Johnny be 'Put away your toys,' and have Johnny answer back 'No, I won't. I hate you!'"

"They didn't talk about this in Lamaze," adds Samalin, who holds a master's degree in counseling and was a protégée of the late Haim Ginott. She envisions parenting courses and workshops as an extension of prenatal training and feels that everyone should enroll.

"Parenting education is relatively new," she says, "but look at it this way: Twenty years ago, prenatal classes were not accepted. Now it's expected. You've spent all this time preparing for the birth. Now what? Nobody tells you your kid will drive you bananas. You're not prepared. The more parent support groups, the less guilty and the more empowered these parents are going to feel." (They must feel pretty empowered, then; a recent edition of *The Big Apple Parents' Paper* ran about a dozen adds for such groups.)

"The population I attract is used to being strong, prepared; they're above-average people. And I'll tell you something," she adds, "what I teach is more important than Suzuki violin"—which a lot of this market buys into as well.

The operative word, though, is teach. The class she has just led came equipped with notepads, ballpoints, three-ring binders. They argued enthusiastically about specialized lectures, other classes; flyers were passed around, heads bent down, and hands set to scribbling. "Have you taken Turecki? No, but have *you* caught Taffel's lecture?" There was a slight air of anxiety, as though Samalin might throw a pop quiz.

Samalin had, in fact assigned "homework." Parents dug into their satchels, pulling out "bug" lists (what they disliked about their kids) and "brag" lists (what they liked). Everyone came prepared with "dialogues," faithful renditions of recent family dramas. Since this group's progeny had a median age of around eleven, these were far from dull. "My son just told me to *fuck off*," said one mother, feistiness and pleasure blending with the Brooklyn in her voice. "Hey, I was ready for it: I socked him before he knew what was happening. Wham!" Her hand gesticulates, bangles jangling, ten red-tipped fingers swatting at the air.

Samalin, who prides herself on never criticizing parents, simply wants to know what others think of this. Nobody goes too crazy about thwacking a bratty preteen. They've been there; they've been everywhere. Nothing could shock them. One mother's son, though an "A" student, gets blinding migraines, another's has a problem with obesity (he sees two professionals; his mother sees Samalin). Subtexts of family misery are hinted at: neglectful husbands, pleasureless childhoods, jealousy between mother and child.

Samalin doesn't pry. "We're not here to psychoanalyze each other," she tells the class, some of whom, "trained" by years of attending these groups, would love to give it a shot. She sticks to her main principles: Choose your battles. Set limits. When parents come close to tears, Samalin brings them back to the brink with comments like "So, she's a pretty good kid, all in all, right?" And mothers nod, smiling, eyes brimming: "Yeah, I guess she is."

There is one lone man in the group. Dressed in business clothes, he offers a joke: "What do you call a bunch of mothers talking in the basement?" Answer: A whine cellar.

"These women basically drive themselves crazy," says Dr. Susan Ginsberg, Associate Dean and Director of the Work and Family Seminars at Bank Street College (and publisher of a corporate parenting newsletter). Like Schulman, Ginsberg offers a comparative perspective of high- and low-income parents, noting that critical times coincide for both groups (both call for help when their children start saying no: toddlerhood and teenhood). She is more impressed, however, by the uniqueness of the privileged parent: "There is something special about the overeducated mother," she says. "The book reader. The class taker."

"They're *so* introspective, so analytical," says Ginsberg. "They write things down and brood about them. It's hard for them not to question themselves; they're so ambivalent about all the different theories." (One mother admits, "It's a catch-22. We want our children to be happy and neurosis-free. But often it's our own compulsion that makes us do all this.") "If there's one thing I taught the mothers at an upper-class, yuppified nursery," says Ginsberg, "it's to stop pussyfooting around."

She continues: "You have to do things with a certain amount of conviction and no backtracking. It's especially hard with working parents," she adds, noting that "a very bright psychologist, no less, let her child kick her. Hard! That woman said everything to that child but *NO*."

There is, among many of the parenting experts, a subtext of bias against working mothers. (Not so against fathers, who are merely given extra credit if they show any interest in the home, becoming, as Ginsberg calls it, "Kramerized.") To exaggerate the caricature, it would be that of harried, ambitious women without the faintest idea of what children really need (somewhat like early Diane Keaton in *Baby Boom,* before she moved to Vermont and started mashing apples). Many decry the reliance on housekeepers, who may or may not be transmitting their employers' values, setting limits, or—a conundrum of their very presence—illustrating social equality.

"People are going to have to deal with this," says one prominent female psychiatrist. "Every child in my neighborhood is being wheeled to the playground by a black or Hispanic woman—whose own child probably lives in worse circumstances. How do you justify that morality? You can start by treating people with respect and love, but there are issues beyond that that have to weigh on your conscience." Sandra Mann, too, is troubled by the absence of real mothering and fathering during the day. "Parenting is a primary prevention program," she says. "What happens in the first five years is more important than anything. So if all you do is get paid help, and worse—put your kids into early programs, the way a lot of ambitious parents do, forcing them to separate, to negotiate the environment before they can handle it—you may see problems later." Mann insists that "children suffer terribly from not having Mother or Father with them at home. You can't learn to love unless you've been really loved."

Ginsberg, though, is far more sanguine about the picture of modern urban women: "On the contrary, I think mothers working *helps* children. Working parents are that much less hovering, less obsessive about parenthood," she says, citing as an example that stay-at-home (but erstwhile fast-track) mothers may crowd the child as he does his homework. "They have to check that everything is perfect." Moreover, says Ginsberg, "working mothers set a wonderful example for their children." She speaks from experience: Both her daughters are now mental-health professionals. "And," she says, "I see nothing wrong with hiring someone good to help you out, assuming you treat them professionally." This is no small task for insecure mothers, who may doubt the "professionality" of their own, delegated role.

Bibliophilia may help shore up the frail prenatal ego, processing parenthood—and childhood—into subdivisible "themes" laid out in black and white. When I visit the prominent New York children's bookstore, Eeyore's, Steve Geck, the West Side store's manager, and Joel Fram, the owner, are barraged by questions from demanding, savvy parents. "Do you have a book that has a funny ending but no silly rhymes or nonsense words and isn't frightening?" shouts one mother, who leads her meek three-year-old by the hand. "Anything on grandparents getting sick?" asks another. "We *have* to get something on sharing," pleads a third. "And I mean, right *now, today.*"

Retreating to a sanctuary below the fray, Geck notes that parents lately seem to want more books about "tough issues." "More writers are imaginatively addressing the problems of old age and infirmity on a level that children can understand," adds Fram. Both see a demand for books on feelings and individuality, books that counter racism, books that deal with pressures to conform. But we don't sell many "preachy" books, says the owner, who much prefers imaginative stories, fairy tales, and fables. Sharon Hancock, manager of Eeyore's East Side store adds, "If we see a book with a title like *Lying* and a subtitle like *Teach Me to Be Good,* it's going to end up the remainder table here on the East Coast. Though I hear they sell in the South like crazy."

Curious about why such books sell *anywhere* like crazy, I try to talk to Joy Berry, founder of the "Human Race Club" (an imprint of the Living Skills Press). She is hard to pin down on the phone, canceling a number of appointments, then launching abruptly into a practiced, hard-sell precis of her company's tactics: "I publish over two-hundred-fifty self-help books," she asserts. "That adds up to *over forty-two million books* sold on the market." Figures and money kept coming up; it is hard to get back to any other publishing motive.

"Look," she says, covering that point. "I was a teacher, I was a principal. I was disillusioned with the educational system in this country. I didn't think it turned people into good people, healthy people, whatever.

"Before we invented 'self-help,' people kept using fantasy, you know, stories and fairy tales. Well, what do you want to accomplish: Do you want to entertain, or do you want to modify behavior? We want to modify behavior."

It appeared she had never read—or had been unimpressed by—Bruno Bettelheim's watershed book *The Uses of Enchantment,* in which he redeemed fairy tales' value in addressing the deepest questions of childhood. In explaining the etiology of moral behavior, Bettelheim says that when a child reads fairy tales, he "identifies with the good hero not because of his goodness, but because the hero's condition makes a deep positive appeal to him. The question for the child is not 'Do I want to be good?' but 'Who do I want to be like?'" By contrast, books that "[tell] the child what to do just replac[e] the bondage of his own immaturity with the bondage of servitude to the dicta of adults."

The child, says Bettelheim, "needs to be encouraged to engage in fantasies," even fantasies of cruelty and revenge. To deny him that right, he says, may be to court danger in adolescence: ". . . deprived of [fantasy] prematurely in childhood, through stark reality having been forced upon [them] . . . young people feel that now is their last chance to make up for a severe deficiency in their life experience, or that without having had a period of belief in magic, they will be unable to meet the rigors of adult life. *Many people who today seek escape in drug-induced dreams, apprentice themselves to some guru . . . engage in practicing 'black magic,' or who in some other fashion escape from reality into daydreams . . . were prematurely pressed to view reality in an adult way.*" [My emphasis.]

"There are only two ways to modify behavior," Joy Berry continues, a cold shower after the warm bath of Bettelheim. "Through story, or through didactic method. We choose the didactic method. Say you want your child to do something. The *worst* way is to tell some story about it. You can bring in ducks and elephants until the cows come home, but it won't be the same as saying, 'Okay, this is how you do it. Step one, two, three.' It's all skill—like making friends."

Responding to the question of why parents couldn't help guide their children, Berry laughed. "Parents? Most parents don't know how to act themselves. They perpetuate the ignorance." Then came the marketer's coup de grace: "Besides, children are not that responsive to their parents. But if a book says so, it must be so."

* * *

"I've read every book there is, practically," says one woman, once a vice president at Goldman Sachs on Wall Street. Since her child's birth, nearly two years ago, she has attended dozens of seminars at New York Hospital, the Babies Club at Lenox Hill, and the Y, where she is registered full time in the Parenting Center. She also attends the Early Childhood Development Center, where Dr. Nina Lief, grande dame of parent facilitators, presides. "Everyone in class is in awe of her," she laughs. "I'm not; I've read too much to swallow anything totally." As proof of her nerve, this mother is pregnant with her second child, pregnant even though Lief has told everyone *not* to space children any closer than three years apart.

"I *do* hide the pregnancy, though," she tells me, rushing her words. "And so does this other woman, Terry. You should see us wearing our big shirts, holding big bags in front of our stomachs, so that Dr. Lief doesn't suspect we've betrayed her." Didn't she think Lief was right about the three-year spacing idea (which sounds like the Burton White line)? "Oh, who knows?" she says, uncharacteristically breezy, "you get pregnant when you get pregnant."

"You know, you can read Leach, Bettelheim, Brazelton, all those experts, and they *still* don't directly answer all your questions," she continues. "So I also get some newsletters, and I subscribe to a bunch of parenting magazines. But that's not enough either. My baby was getting more and more assertive, and no matter what I learned, I had no idea what to do until, finally, a friend told me that these workshops were the answer. They are, for the time being. When Annie gets older, we'll probably go to classes together, something to prepare us for nursery school."

"I miss my job at Goldman," she confides. "I'm *definitely* going back, sometime. But now I'm really into the classes and child thing. At times it becomes absolutely like being busy on Wall Street.

"I have a friend who used to be at Kidder Peabody. She's doing the same thing; classes and seminars, books and workshops. We laugh about how we analyze and scrutinize the issues—it's exactly like we're working. We even have our little networks of mothers, just like we used to have networks of business acquaintances. Someone will call up and say, 'I took Course X,' and she'll fill me in on what she knows. And I can fill her in on Course Y. In fact, some of my friends—who don't research all this stuff—are amazed, impressed, by what I can tell them. They'll say, 'How did you know that?' I tell them I got it from this seminar or that."

"I have been there," says Samalin, referring to the lost, searching quality of modern parenthood. "I used to know *nothing* but nagging-yelling-pleading-criticizing-arguing-and-punishing." Sign up with the experts, she implies, and be free. "I tell them—and it's certainly been true for me—'The good thing about parenthood is that, one way or another, you *always* get another chance to show what you learned.'"

TWENTY-THREE

SCHOOLTIME FOR BABY

As there is never any consensus about what is good for your child, the decision as to whether, where, and when to enroll her in preschool is bound to be tense. It ought to be.

For many children, their first formal encounter with the world outside the home will happen when they are as young as two. As someone pointed out to me, that means that these kids will have had four years of schooling—the equivalent of a college diploma—before they hit first grade.

In New York, and I suspect in most urban centers, mothers sit on park benches during the dog days of summer, swatting wasps away from the apple juice, and plotting their child's entry into the world of organized play, snack, and separation.

Separation? Emma had just turned two. She still had that round little potbelly, her hair was wispy, soft, and fair. Did they say separation?

Trying to escape the pressure, I called two friends whose children are older than mine. Both told me that of _course_ they sent their kids, at two, to preschool. The kids, they concurred, had a blast. One, a boy, had become avid about finger painting. The other, a girl, had become obsessed with nature—"in a good way, you know, she knew about seeds and why leaves fall off trees."

I was feeling only the simple wish to keep my small leaf stuck to my tree. For a little while longer.

"No, no," said the first friend. "She'll go crazy at home!"

"She'll climb the walls," said the other.

"And so will you," whispered the first.

School was described as freedom, mutual freedom. Home was the cage, jail, and the thought of keeping a child there, neurotic, clinging, compulsive.

Still, I felt rebellious. Why *should* she leave home? I thought. What was everyone running after? I'd read a bit of David Elkind et al. in my time; these compulsive reading habits can come in handy when you're trying to back up your gut instinct.

In my fortunate case, as well as the case of most of these bench mothers, there was someone at home for the child, either I or my house-keeper. We didn't need day care. These parents were looking for an enrichment program for their kids, but I couldn't see how being in class would be so enriching as to outdo home, hearth, and the occasional play-date. I mean, was it merely a matter of buying a good easel and a smock?

Still, as my friend had explained to me, they learn to be in school from being in school (a great tautology); by three they're expected to know how to "act" among their peers; this will be looked for in future applications to future schools. (And application for preschool for three-year-olds would begin any minute.) I began to feel like the rabbit in *Alice in Wonderland,* nervously winding my existential watch, always late for a very important (but possibly meaningless) date.

Then, too, as we have seen, I had become pregnant sometime in Emma's second year, and had given birth one month before her second birthday. Suddenly, I was struggling to take care of an infant and a two-year-old at the same time, both high need, and trying to do it without losing my perspective, poise, or looks. (That latter point isn't whimsy—if I didn't get to the gym, and soon, I was in danger of becoming a prehis-toric fertility totem.)

It *would* be easier, I gradually came to think, to take one child to school some mornings a week, leaving the other alone with me. After all, shouldn't second children have it as good as the first? (I'm a second child and have thought hard about these inequities.) If Gabriel's morning nap remained consistent, I mused, I might even be able to squeeze some exercise into the morning, instead of sitting through the duller parts of

Mr. Rogers with Emma. And wouldn't it do Emma some good to be out of the house, away from the duller parts of Mr. Rogers and, more important, away from Baby? She'd find a peer group, to which the little usurper did not belong. She'd make drawings that I'd hang on the fridge, and return, invigorated, to the hearth I always talk about.

Then there was the touchy matter of her recent behavior. While every day before the birth she had become sweeter and sweeter, touching my growing belly, saying "baby in dere," now, sheer rebellion had overtaken her. Something began to simmer in me when she began acting angry, aggressive, and at times unrecognizably nasty. I take everyone altogether too seriously, and my children head that list. That's not always a good thing. Sadness, and madness, sometimes come of scrutinizing things too seriously, or—worse—too personally.

A brief diversion on the nature of personal preferences and the raising of children, a subject universally shunned as taboo, and one that complicates decision such as whether or not to see less of the child who wounds you.

This touches on the even touchier subject of my cheating heart, which began its straying path the minute I gave birth for the second time.

There is nothing, they say, like first love, until you have another child. God Himself started playing favorites the moment there was not only Cain but Abel. But we mortals seem to dwell on the puzzle of multiple loyalties, guilty each time we prefer the company of one child over another. And we do, inevitably, shift alliances. There was a time, not too long ago, when I favored newborn Gabriel over his strong-willed older sister. It's just that no one is supposed to admit this.

My own father favored me. I made him, a taciturn man, laugh long and loud. I made him proud. I knew how to sit still. I was curious about the right things (science, God), and not about the wrong (his lack of hair). And I looked like his mother, deceased; I carried her name. Still, it has taken years for him to own up to the preference.

Here is what happened to me. First I gave birth to Emma, my first love, a Monday's child. Fair like her father, from the moment of birth, Emma has been a dazzling rambunctious spirit on whom nothing is lost. Emma is such an original that all I wanted to do was shower her with everything—including a sibling. By the time she turned two, she got the gift of Gabriel.

By two, read "terrible two." Some powerful convergence of age and opportunity created Terrible, Terrible Two. Emma the inimitable became Emma the quite frightful (I'd forget the potbelly, the soft yellow hair). Her eyes were vigilant, and hurt. Nothing being lost on her meant that she saw every loving gesture I made to the new baby, every glance, every sigh. To which she responded with long, sirenlike shrieks. Suddenly, Emma seemed sullen sixteen—and dangerous.

Gabriel, for his part, did what a certain mythical type of neonate does. He looked out at me from his bassinet, sloe eyes seeking mine for a melting stare. From a woman who felt she could never love again, I felt like a woman possessed by the Love Demon.

That my second child was a boy, a fact that seemed odd and un-Emma-like at first, now seemed the very thing. He was my boy. My brave little fella. I was his mother, and he was my son. I was the Madonna, and he was the Child. We entered into a poignant, tranquil scene, punctuated by the crazy screams and unpredictable, powerful tantrums of Emma.

My poor girl. Even as I write this, and even as it happened—not so long ago—I knew that all she wanted was me, all alone, to herself. And often, what I wanted—it hurts me, for her sake, to confess it—was to have Gabriel, all alone, to myself. For the first few months of his life, Emma's brother was put down, virtually in hiding, to appease the sad hunger that had taken over my girl.

Often, she wouldn't be appeased. No, she was angry; she hated me. When I opened my arms to her, she'd run away, screaming (always factor in that screaming). And when her hatred was especially dark—two-year-olds are formidable in their sometime darkness—she brought out of me an echoing negativity, which seemed to gladden her in an odd way. I think there are moments, sometimes entire stages, when any child can be hard to love, times when only patience, politeness, or the most basic parental instinct is forced to kick in.

Motherly shame at my own subversive thoughts made it worse. In my madness, partly hormonal, I wept. And I'd even wonder why she didn't know that I was hurting, too. Answer: Because she's two, two, two, and she's going to be acting like this for quite a while. Sylvia Plath was beginning to make sense to me.

Weekends were strange. She'd have her father then, and she'd cling to him, and I'd hold Gabriel, and we'd seem like a unit only to strangers. Prideful, she'd watch me from beneath hooded eyes, and if I wanted to cuddle her, she'd usually say, *"No."*

Until the day she rode the horse.

The horse was not a real horse. It was a mechanical horse, the sort that rides for about a minute, to the tune of *The William Tell Overture*, for the price of a quarter. Our horse was situated in front of a store called Wings, making it a Pegasus sort of horse, in a way. Week after week, Emma would look at the horse, then at my husband, then—from under those lids—at me. And we'd say, Emma, would you like to take a ride? And she'd say *"No,"* and we'd keep going.

That day, a sunny Sunday, Emma was wearing a raincoat she'd refused to take off since the rainy day we'd made her wear it. That day was also the tenth day of her milk strike. She'd gone back to drinking from a bottle to be more like Gabriel, only we'd given her the wrong one (she'd broken the right one by hurling it to the ground), and now she was mad, real mad.

Gabriel lay sleeping in his carriage as Emma eyed the horse. Finally, she muttered, "Wanna ride horse right now." Without thinking much about it, my husband hoisted her up. She looked small on the horse, her feet barely making it into the metal stirrups. She leaned forward and grabbed the horse under his cold neck, her cheek touching his. Then she looked up abruptly. The music had started, and the horse was moving.

She looked at me. She was proud. I saw that she was also frightened; her body never changed position, as though she felt that the slightest thing could topple her. In that moment, I knew that although my love for Emma had seemed to waver, it had never fallen off. It wouldn't fall off for anything or anyone.

We saw each other. I saw my girl, the only girl in a raincoat that warm Sunday, scared but smiling, proud and traveling. And I thought, My girl is flying on Pegasus, but she's still right there by my side. Thank God, I thought, that moving horse isn't going anywhere. Because there's nothing on earth more beloved to me, and I want her here, right here.

And she saw me and knew what I knew.

Once that ambivalence was gone, paradoxically, I could think again of sending her away. It's not boarding school, said my husband, the

Englishman. It's not Eton! And, I thought, practically, school may be
just the thing to temporize this domestic *Sturm und Drang.*

We found a school in the neighborhood—the only one with spaces
available in August! Still, it wasn't bad at all. It was three blocks away,
up a pleasant avenue. The schoolroom housed a rabbit, good vibes, and
a lanky, able head teacher. Lots of toys were cleverly stashed in a tidy
space as small as a rabbit's warren. As summer school was in session,
(this school was open year-round), we were able to observe everyone in
action. The little children, having had what schools like to call a nutri-
tious snack (rice cake and peanut butter), got up and cleared their own
mess. The scene was not out of Oliver Twist—my biggest nightmare.

Paul and I, observing, soberly agreed that we'd go to that school
ourselves, if they'd admit us. Even though together, we had already accu-
mulated about a half-century of education, and by rights should have
been burned out, we stuck around at the school, imagining what it was
like to be a kid again. (Some experts say that's how you choose a school:
Imagine if you'd like to attend it yourself.) We became effusive with the
director, letting her know our relief at finding such a wonderful place.
She seemed flattered, although she did not offer us rice cake.

In fact, one tiny part of our consciousnesses factored in the information that the director seemed a bit rigid. Her response to us had the
flavor of those telephone solicitations in which you are read a programmed script with little intonation. And the script is read regardless
of response, like a human tape loop. Too, Patricia had a painted smile,
a fruit-slice mouth. But there was hope: She was pregnant, very (always
a humanizing factor), her maternity dress summery, sleeveless, pumpkin-
colored. We felt that with the advent of motherhood, Patricia would
unleash more of her pumpkin side, and that her phone-tape aspects
would diminish.

Patricia confided that due to our "lateness" in application, we would
have to decide quickly. Space for September *was* filling up! She certainly
didn't want to have "the situation we had last year, with parents fighting
in the halls." Fighting in the halls! Paul and I, too, did not want that.
(We don't believe in violence, particularly in front of impressionable
children.)

So we signed up immediately. Gratefully.

There was one more thing. Patricia told us that all the kids who
attended in the morning would "need to" attend five days a week, be-

cause they adjust better that way. I felt that two or three mornings were ample for my toddler, not to mention for me. (I would miss her.) Most preschools, by the way, do offer the choice. I checked that out in my *Pre-School Handbook,* which also explained that separation is a process that should be handled delicately, because some children don't go for leaving Mom, home, and comfort behind and entering the ranks of con- formity. I think it may have something to do with the fact that they are, after all, children.

Anyway, Patricia's tape loop was patiently telling me, repeating to me, that five days is best, that they thrive on five. There was that pre- dictability factor to consider, she said. Two-year-olds like structure. Be- sides, she added (an aside), it's more convenient for us as a group.

Group dynamics. Suddenly, this was turning into a social-science experiment, the one in which you buckle down to peer pressure (the very thing you hope your kids won't easily do.) Danger signal, overlooked by us two pressured rubes. We signed.

I still had misgivings—this is so *typical* of us parents—but the thought of Emma having a rabbit to pet and avoiding the sight of us fighting in the halls for a school space (at least until the prep school years) consoled me, mildly—like a weak sedative, a glass of sherry. The kids in the class did seem happy (the year was ending; most of them had turned three, some four). I told Emma she was going to school soon, and she seemed really excited about it.

I, on the other hand, at the parent's orientation a few weeks later felt the proverbial pit-of-the-stomach feeling. I wanted to cry, but like a child who feared the shame of crying, I tried not to. My effort was enhanced by Patricia telling us that sometimes it's the parent who has a problem separating. I didn't want Patricia to see how weak, how prob- lematic, I was.

Patricia had spoken about other things, too. A parent whose child was enrolled in the older—three-to-four-year-old—class found out that a good teacher was not coming back. She said that had she'd known that, she'd not have returned, and since Patricia had known for a while, she accused Patricia of tricking her. Smiling mechanically but enunciating patiently, Patricia answered that everything would be fine. Why did the teacher leave? insisted the parent.

She didn't appreciate, as I now do, that the job is grueling, the pay shameful, and hence, the turnover great. I later learned that Patricia had simply decided not to give the teacher in question the raise she wanted. A not-atypical move.

When another parent wondered who would take charge when Patricia took maternity leave, we were introduced to Wendy, a shy woman with invisible eyelashes. Her shyness lifted my spirits. I suspected that Wendy, being new, temporary, and a bit human, would respond to my fears, maybe even let Emma have the forbidden part-time schedule.

I was still brooding about having Emma in school five days a week, five long mornings that included, for some reason, lunch. I thought lunch was an intimate, cozy time for a small child. A hot noodle-soup time, a silly sounds and faces time that preceded deep-nap time. I looked around for other parents to brood with about the general excessiveness of the program, but most wanted to know if they could leave their kids for longer periods of time. Parents of two-year-olds were scarce, in any case. (So much for the fighting-in-the-hall routine.) Emma would be one of only three two-year-olds (the other children in her class were a year older). One of those toddlers, Stacy, had a special inside deal allowing her to attend only on Mondays and Fridays.

Learning of the special inside deal, I stared again at the interim director. Yes, I thought, bad rules are made to be broken, and we, too, may strike a deal. My brows and lashes were darker than hers; I felt powerful.

On behalf of my child, who is incredibly verbal and funny, but at times coherent only to me and my housekeeper, I planned to be the most vigilant, strongest, deal-striking mother ever hardened by fire.

And then I stepped out and I cried. My brain was Machiavellian, planning, improving, seeing things through to their practical end. My gut was maternal: I didn't want this for my baby!

In part, this is a book about going by the maternal gut.

The reason this book exists is that we rarely do.

My gut suddenly didn't like another thing about the school. I had learned, in a postmeeting huddle, that the school encouraged kids to separate by having the mothers sit outside the classroom, and *never step inside*. A child had this choice: Sit outside with Mother, or come in alone and play with the others. This further rigidity, however logical, made me wince. Did that mean that if Emma said, Mommy, *come*, that I'd have to say, No, you must go there; I must stay here? I thought it might go better if I did step inside for a day or so, then slowly amble out when she calmed down.

My husband felt differently. Emma'll love it; she's so incredibly active. Louise Bates Ames and Frances Ilg, authorities on the two-year-old, think "a good nursery school" is just the thing for active, sociable twos and their tired elders. And the clincher: In the park, said my husband, doesn't she always chase groups of kids around saying "friends, friends!"?

It was true. She always followed the school groups around and tried to drink their juice.

Paul also reminded me that, with Emma in school, I could finally get to see Gabriel alone. Not only that, I'd have more time to work, go to the gym, and see people. You know, adult people, business colleagues, friends, and combinations, the way he gets to do. The way I used to do.

Yes, it sounded good, provided no one had to suffer.

My number-one rule of motherhood at the time (the rule that everyone who knows mothers seems to ruthlessly prey upon) was, above all, no needless suffering. Later, I substituted the medical maxim: Above all, do no harm. Sometimes they come to the same thing.

But would Emma suffer? Of course not, said my father, who was big on fortitude and goals for girls and boys. Raised in a poor home, he added, "She's *lucky* to go to school! Look at all those resources she'll be exposed to!" Given the price of attendance, that seemed a plausible argument. Not everyone, clearly, can afford to send their kid to preschool. By definition, I guess that means it is a luxury, like zebra steak.

Yale Law School is also a luxury. I mention it because I went there, and I had the worst time of my life. (No fault of Yale's; simply a monumental mismatch.) My father used to say not everyone could get in there, and it was absolutely true. I'd felt as though I'd received an expensive, rare, and unwanted gift. A white elephant, with (from my perspective) massive droppings to be shoveled from my path.

I took my child to school, suspiciously, vigilantly. I looked for signs of her luckiness all around. Yes, the rabbit was still there, alive. "Blackie," the kids call him. Kind of a roguish, lucky name. Howya doin' there, Blackie? Emma knelt down and tried to feed him a blade of straw.

Blackie was there, but teacher migration (due to bad pay) being the norm, the one I'd admired on first viewing the school had now moved into the class for older threes and fours. The new one, Emma's, was called Fern, and looked it.

Fern was neither lanky nor easygoing. Facing her group of squirming tinies, she had the manner of a novice bicyclist, grip too tight on the hand brakes. (Her lethargic assistant, on the other hand, was no great comfort either.) Facing me, on one of the most emotionally wrenching days of my life, she used jargon like "age appropriate" and "large motor." Almost as bad, she called me *Mrs.* Taitz, though Emma's surname is not Taitz.

Fern bucked defensively when I asked if she'd had a lot of experience with two-year-olds before. I asked because she looked so tense, so ready to withstand. Two-year-olds need a bit of humor and flow-state charisma. "Yes, for a summer," she snapped. "I know the twenty-four-month profile. Oppositionality."

That means she knows that two-year-olds say "no" before "yes," so that, for instance, if you ask them if they've had a bowel movement, they tend to say "no" when they have. But when, en route to the roof for her "large motor" activity, Emma passed me, I realized that she was soaking wet and soiled to the waistband. "Do you need your diaper changed?" I asked. "Poo-poo," she honestly answered.

Fern told me that she had just *asked* Emma "if she needed to go to the toilet," but that Emma had said "no." (Oppositionality, Fern.) I suggested that it might be time to change her now. Summer school or not, I noted, Fern had never seen a diaper before. She had never seen a preschool diaper table, with its theoretically changeable paper lining, before. And she seemed, certainly, never to have seen a two-year-old's huge opus before, smashed and blossoming.

I saw her try to assimilate it all, sight, smell, the mammoth wipe-job ahead of her, but she could not, and swayed infinitesimally backward.

She did not know which end of the diaper was up, whether or how to change that table's liner paper, whether or how to wash her hands without losing the other (doubtless equally soiled) twos to chaos. She acquited herself quickly, not washing her hands, changing the paper, or checking the others.

Small details, you say? Not anymore, not to me.

I also noticed that the school soap, a pump antibacterial, was diluted. I added that to my list of grievances.

I suppose I am a preschool's nightmare mom, Cher in *Mask*, a harridan, but, I think, too bad. Here is where that Yale Law training finally comes in. I am Emma's advocate, her pro bono angel.

All this was real, but it was also, of course, metaphorical. My bottom-line fear was that Emma would not be taken care of in her helplessness. If they can't even clean her bum, how would they approach her complex personality?—now made troublesome by the arrival of a brother. If they can't handle her body in the right way, how would they love *her* enough or in the right way?

An elaborate, singular personality was housed in that two-year-old shell. Her exuberance, tempered by sudden gentleness. Her utter refusal to do things when and the way she was told. Her humor, her word-play, her million expressions, the thundering wet raspberry she gave to new acquaintances. Her utter belief in friendship, and her hurt look when things went awry between people, even subtle things.

Over and over, an analogy of child in preschool/parent in nursing home kept occurring to me. I would not want my helpless parent improperly changed, inadequately loved, unknown.

With a child, there is an extra, painful factor. This was Emma's first contact not only with school, but with the outside world. With life as most of us adults now know it. Who would be bending my little twig, in what direction, and with what intention or what careless lack of intention?

No parent seemed to mind or notice any of the things I've mentioned. I say this not out of any sense of virtue, but out of puzzlement, and some hurt. Perhaps I, like Emma, was too complex to fit in, too microcalibrated, too reactive. Even so, my vigilance felt right. If Emma was in the wrong hands, how would she be able to tell me? She wouldn't know, and couldn't tell me if she did. And they, the ham fists, certainly would neither know nor tell me.

Was this like Baby-Sitter-Land, which some mothers prefer not to explore too closely? I have rarely met a mother who didn't think the sitter was a "treasure," until the firing (after some appalling revelation) or the shock of being left. Most likely, it was a question of assumed competence, fueled by a *need* to make that assumption. Schools and day-care centers are supposed to know children and hire well. If they don't, the mother's world gets nightmarish. There is also a subtle form of "we know what's best for you" pressure that makes smart people dumb. Who are we to second-guess the principal?

The parents, that's who. The ones who know most, love most, and will have to live, forever, with the results of whatever experiment is in progress on our children.

My second-guessing was focused, for the moment, on germs. They seemed a concrete analogue to my fear of external contaminants to the child I love and want the world to embrace. My recent new motherhood, the baby boy at home, contributed to that fear. I thought that in a school where new teachers had not been indoctrinated about the use of soap, undiluted soap, anything could happen.

Emma could get sick here, I thought, and then, Gabriel. At the time, he was only three months old. At home, we were all Dial-soapers. The teacher's fumbling routine around the diaper table made me worry about him as well as his sister.

Almost as soon as my rational counterdebater voice told me to cool it, stop doing a Howard Hughes routine, Emma got sick. (She'd been at school for eight days.) She got so acutely, screamingly sick that no painkiller killed the pain she was in. We shot infant Tylenol down her throat, half of it dribbling out of her open, sobbing mouth and down her wobbling chin. The mouth and chin dripped not only Tylenol but blood. Emma was suddenly, inexplicably, bleeding.

There is nothing more chilling than the sight of your child's blood. Emma had developed an odd, persistent ailment that caused her gums to ache, soften, and release a slow stream of red between her teeth. She got sores on her lower lip, too. But for her writhing away from the painkiller, she hardly had the energy to move. That, too, was new to us, and awful.

I took her to the doctor, one of four in a group practice. He said it was "stomatitis." I looked up the word. It means inflammation of the mouth. Her condition worsened. I called the practice and got another doctor who told me she had Coxsackie, or hand, foot, and mouth disease. It's funny, the name; everyone calls it hoof-and-mouth, ha ha. But I'd completely lost my sense of humor in the face of a screaming child whose mouth hurt whenever she ate—she'd put an appalled hand to it after a bite, look at me in beseeching terror, and wail unappeasably.

I told him it couldn't be Coxsackie; her hands and feet were not involved. He told me they don't have to be. Still another doctor, on a repeat visit, suggested that Emma may have caught oral herpes somewhere. That's it, I thought. That's the last straw. No more school.

Voice low, serious, I said to the doctor, I shouldn't have sent her; now she's got something permanent, incurable, painful. To which he responded, Hey they all get things the minute they go to school. "Don't panic," he said. "It's not genital herpes—it's just cold sores. Everyone gets them, haven't you?"

"No," I said.

I asked him why she'd been so sick for so long. Why she'd been so tired. Why a child who never kept still and was always up to something interesting was now listless—when not sobbing and bleeding from the mouth. He said, I really don't know what's wrong with her. If it goes on much longer, we'll "do some tests."

That scared me, of course. I said, Tests? What are you testing for? He was silent. He should have reassured me that most things are nothing—at least nothing deadly—but he didn't. So I said, Oh, come on, what are you saying—you'd test her for—for cancer? He said, Yeah, maybe. But you said it's probably just a virus, I said. Oh, who knows, he said. Yeah, probably. Let's just keep an eye on her. As though I'd taken my eye off her for the last many weeks.

As we spoke, I started to feel that all this incurable pain seemed very much like the fall from grace, like the booting out of Eden. Where was this coming from? I'm no believer in original sin, but then, this wasn't original sin; it was brought on, contracted, passed on by some snaky germ, by a teacher who didn't wash her hands, by a school that didn't care, didn't mind, didn't *love*. By me, who wanted her out of the house, who hurried her to grow up and make my life easier. Who wanted Gabriel alone, to be my next dream child, without the rude intrusion of a nay-saying two-year-old. And now blood had intruded. Blood, pain, and fear of death.

I thought about how Gabriel could catch whatever it was, too. He was so little, so pure. His hair was softer than the feathers of the smallest bird. When a bit of city soot—a dot no bigger than a pinpoint—fell on his face, I stared at its incongruity. How did it dare land on my silken angel? Even wiping it off abraded his cheek, made it pink.

I thought about the whole world outside my home, polluting forever my two perfect children. When I told people about how I felt they told me to get more sleep. Of course. I was up day and night with screaming Emma and hungry Gabriel (where are you now, Nurse Nicole?), but that's not all of it. There is fatigue, and there is mother's mania, and there is my own specific mania, but there is also something more. The world cannot be kept sterile, and strangers can't be mothers, but some schools, still, are stinking rotten, and something should be done about it.

My husband was sympathetic to my feelings about the school. It's not that he felt particularly angry at it. He is rarely angry; he is equable, sane, and optimistic. Tending to think that everyone does his best (as *he* does), he will turn the other cheek, time and again. But he loved me enough to take a good look at my burning red face and take my side.

He agreed that the hygiene had not been optimal. Emma was one of only three toddlers, as I've said, and the third one part time. The other children were older, and toilet-trained. There were two teachers there to take care of them. And shouldn't they have called, I said, after all this time, to see how she is? Isn't it rare, I said, that a kid is out, week after week, and school has barely started? Don't they wonder—or does this sort of thing happen all the time?

I was working up my spitfire closing argument, when *he* called the school. He told the head teacher that Emma was really quite ill. He told them that she must have caught something, but that the doctors weren't sure if it was Coxsackie, cold sores, or stomatitis. They *thought* it was viral, he said, but if she does not get better, they are going to run tests. Fern listened.

He told them that Emma's mother was by now exhausted, and raw-nerved, and that it might be nice to give her a call.

Fern now spoke. She was formal and polite. She said she was sorry to hear that Emma was unwell. She asked when it would be best to call Mrs. Taitz. He told her when. She called me.

When I heard her voice on the telephone, I felt relieved. Emma and I up to then, had been cut off from the intense experience we so recently began. Now I could talk to someone who knew what was going on in school, who might—ideally—be able to deal with whatever may have caused this problem.

"Do you think it was the diluted soap?" I said, sounding crazy, I suppose. A monomaniac with a soap fetish. "Because, you know, it was diluted. Also, it might be good if 'they' could change the changing-table paper after each use, so that germs aren't spread." Then, quickly, "And do you think the kids ought to get their hands washed from time to time?"

I was using my deferential tone. A real effort.

Fern listened quietly. When I finished, she said:

"Look, I think whatever Emma has, she got from you."

"Could you repeat that?" I felt the thrill of rising rage. I tried to control it.

"I think that Emma didn't get sick at school. I think she probably has a, you know, some people have a genetic, you know, tendency, to get sick a lot, especially with herpes, you know?"

I was beginning to hate this woman.

"Yeah. You two probably have herpes, and so Emma inherited it, see?"

"Fern," I responded, "I think you know little about biology. Even if we had had this virus, you don't inherit viruses. You *catch* them, usually from physical contact. These kids play together in a tiny room. They are diapered together. You're supposed to wash your hands and change the table paper. That's more relevant than our DNA. You're supposed to make *them* wash their hands, after a diaper change and before snack and lunch. *That's* relevant, not the antediluvian condition of my genes."

I used words like "antediluvian" when I am furious, especially when sure that they will intimidate. I was fighting the dirty fight: the fight of the brainy against the idiotic and misinformed. This was not effective.

"And you are supposed to use soap—undiluted soap—to kill the viruses and/or the bacteria. When you don't, *you* are going to catch some flak when children get sick!"

"DON'T YOU DARE YELL AT ME!"

This was the teacher blowing her lid. Suddenly, it occurs to her that I am merely Mrs. Taitz. Hysteric, meany *Mother*. And she, Fern, is a trained professional, with four years of college under her belt, a summer's experience with children, and the potential—should she complete night school—to obtain an M.A. that will make her even more immune to my puny pain.

The fact that *she* was now angry scared me. Yes, I had lost my temper, and I had been nasty, but turning her own argument around, she was the professional, right? I am allowed to get irate; I am the mother. She should have kept a cooler head. It wasn't her child, screaming for relief.

I told her this. I was crying.

"L-look," I said. "I'm upset. My child is really sick. I can't stand it when she cries even for one second, and she's crying—really hard crying—all the time. This has gone on for week after week. She hates the medicine, and even when she gets it down her throat, it doesn't help her. And then there's a baby in the house, too. What's going to happen to him?"

"Calm down," she said coldly. "In my experience, kids get sick all the time."

"They do?"

"Yes. That's what happens at school. It's normal. To be expected."

"So you agree that she caught this at school?"

"No, she got it from you, genetically," said this dork, dictatorially, "and I have to go now."

"Let me tell you one last thing," I told her. "I am tired, and I am worn out, but you are full of bull, especially in the science department, and you had better stop saying what you're saying."

"Are you threatening me?"

I thought about it. I'd have *loved* to threaten her! But I had no power to. Yes, I could have got her fired, but I thought that would be overkill. And maybe I couldn't have got her fired. The school hired this greenhorn. Patricia probably didn't have a vast array of choices. No, it was Fern who had the real power. She was the teacher. She was the one who could treat my daughter badly when I wasn't there to know it.

"No. Look, let's drop this. I'm glad you called, that was nice of you, and Emma will be back soon, and we'll all be happy once more."

Something to that effect.

"She really is a nice kid," said the teacher, surprising me out of my funk.

"Yeah?"

"Yeah. She's real smart. She's real aware. And she has an incredible energy level."

Yeah, she used to, I thought gloomily.

"Thank you," I said obediently.

"I have to get ready for the next shift," she said.

"Okay, 'bye."

"Sure."

"Thanks for calling."

"You're welcome, Mrs. Taitz."

After another week, Emma got better, and I took her back to school.

TWENTY-FOUR

WHEREIN MOM IS JUST A NERVOUS JERK IN THE HALLWAY

y ou sit like a nervous jerk in the hall, and realize that this is worse than the baby-sitter episode. Because here, unlike the world of baby-sitters and their fire-able episodes, the parent goes with the program or the parent goes. It doesn't matter if your two-year-old is not heard when she asks someone, anyone, to tie her shoes. You're sitting in the hall; you hear, but you are not to enter the room. So you wait, in anguish—hell is hearing your child's needs go unan-swered—until one of the teachers has the time or the inclination to help your child, or what was formerly your child, now a ward of the cold, cruel world. A world you would not like to even have lunch with, but that she is going to have lunch with. Cold lunch at a small wooden table.

Mad Dickensian fantasies.

You realize, again, that this is what most of the parents you know are doing, and that some of them have no choice. You realize that America is a country in which at least half of the two-year-olds are eating lunch at preschools, nurseries, and day care centers. You realize that it's crazy that no one is closely supervising this, the way they do in Sweden. You realize with a pang that teachers should be revered, paid more, rewarded for hard experience.

Everyone reassures you, telling you how much kids love it, need it, run to it. You hear somebody else's kid cry. She cries for a long time. You realize that her mother doesn't know the child is crying.

You hope that your child, who sure enough keeps running out to ask you—hope dwindling—to join her in class, is learning patience, sharing, learning. You suspect her teachers of apathy, incompetence, even—under stress—a touch of sharpness. The sort of thing you've stretched and strained for two years, perhaps three, never to surrender to.

You hope, for instance, that if you've never dully said, "I *told* you no," or pinched her arm with anger as you dragged her down the hall, that no one else, however ill paid, will perform those acts on her, and hurt her feelings, or worse, her trust, or worse, her spirit, which sometimes used to drive you crazy. Now, you think miserably, you'd rather have her home running over the sofas with her clackety-clack toy, anything, but not this sterility that is supposed to "separate" you, supposed to teach her social skills and sharing and how to do well throughout life. Now, you think miserably, she is learning that life is two ordinary women in their twenties, who certainly don't love her very much. Why should they?

Few are born to be mothers. I have a horrible, nasty temper that no one but my parents and my husband has ever seen. But certainly my girl—a challenge to the impatient with her boundless energy, intelligence, and desire—has not come across it. When I get angry at her, I control myself. I count, I think of things her way (I know her way because I love her enough to observe her, to mull over her, to see layer under layer of her).

Caught in the force of her volley of will, I make choices. I try to distract her, or I try to make her laugh, or I try to explain why my way is counter to hers, or—quite often, when, as much of life is petty, the particular debate in question is petty—I drop the whole thing. Most of the time we can both save face.

Cowed in the hallway, I thought, I do not want a cowed child, ever. I want one who is happy, cooperative, and goes with the program when the program is good.

Could this program be good? More important, was it any better, or any worse, anywhere else? I had not myself decided, when I heard the assistant teacher sternly telling Emma "NOT TO RUN IN HALLS IT MAKES ME VERY VERY ANGRY."

Running is Emma's very air. She was running because she was happy to be back at school, happy not to be miserably sick anymore. About to show me something, she was running in that hall to me, who sat there because I was told to sit there.

I sat there, listening to the harangue. Emma was not advancing toward me. I imagine that the assistant had physically restrained her. I got sick, angry, and I got up.

Controlling my tone (my anger), I spoke to the assistant about my child. I gave her context. I told her that the best way with Emma—I didn't add, with any child—is through love. That since Emma had been absent and didn't quite know where she was or who she was with, it might be better to engage her cooperation rather than head out for a test of wills.

I should repeat that Emma has the willpower of an Olympic athlete, a hunger striker, an aerialist. She has focus. It isn't easy for the novice to know how to handle her.

Remember, when she didn't get milk in the right bottle, she struck for ten days, at a time when it was milk, milk, milk every minute for the months prior. We still haven't sorted out the milk thing.

Is it all so new? Doesn't anyone train these teachers? *Can* people be trained to become excellent teachers? *Can* they be trained to know—and love—each individual for who he or she is?

"She's having a bad day," said the interim director, referring to the teacher. In my head, the phrase echoed a well-known line from the movie *Crimes of the Heart*. The line that was meant to explain why Mom had to kill herself and the cat.

With such help from the directorship, I felt I should offer some of my own, homespun (deeply unwanted) wisdom.

So I said, "You could tell Emma, 'If you run here, someone could bump you and you'd both get hurt.' She likes reasons," I said. Like everyone else (I didn't say).

Or, I said, "Tell her you want to see if she can march as though in a parade (tell her marching's allowed)."

And I said, "You know what? Tell her she'll be going outside in a little while, for gym time" (or as the school called it, large-muscle-group activity). "And that she can run for an hour, to her heart's delight. Soon."

See what a great, illuminated parent I am? How creative, how well read? So why was I shipping my daughter off, à la Oliver Twist? (That nightmare vision kept returning.)

After class, I brought the "temper" issue—the assistant teacher's, I mean—up again. To her. Very gingerly. Oh, the fear of stepping on a teacher's toes! You wonder if, defensively, they'll take it out on the child when you're not there. Meanwhile you are there, making demands, pleading, so they nod, some of them, tuning you out, tired of this batch and the next.

Me: "She ran around when she wasn't supposed to, huh?"

A brisk nod.

Me again: "Well, she runs a lot at home. She does it most when she's happy." (Get it? I felt like saying. A happy twenty-four-month-old child tends to run rather than walk; she *was* happy before you grabbed her and grunted; and if it bothers you, find another line of work.)

"Maybe you could just sort of start out by getting to know her. She's a little nervous here—" *I* was Oliver Twist, that's who was Oliver Twist. The orphan mother, pleading for a bit more kindness for her child.

She: "Look, there are a lot of kids here—" Yeah, and not much gruel.

"—and she got me real mad."

No apology, no "we got along swell later, don't worry."

Nothing.

She got me real mad, that teacher (though again I pretended to get along swell), but all I could do was take Emma home and smooth her hair and tell her, again, that things are done a certain way in school, usually for a reason.

Welcome to the Institution, mothers and children. Try to fight a bit, politely, fight for the good reason.

Give up, depressed, that you can't make the world a nice place, even though that's what the world, up to now, at least in your domain, has been about.

Stage Two: Realize that you've been a little bit crazy about making the school as so-called "perfect" as your home, that your child is not made of papier-mâché but of sturdy stuff, that she loves school and will do just fine. That the teacher, while no Anne Sullivan, is no Hitler, either, and that her line of work, poorly paid and exhausting, is one none but a saint could do flawlessly.

Stage Three: For God's sake, if you can follow your instinct, get out. That means, if you think she's too young, or she's not in good hands, despite the jargon, the fact that "they thrive on it," and the fact that it does free up your life most wonderfully, maybe you should drop it.

If you can.

TWENTY-FIVE

DROPPING OUT

I couldn't. Not without an arduous process.

The teachers' main goal seemed to be making me leave Emma in their care. Fair enough. But it was hard to leave when my instinct told me not to, when Emma told me not to, and when—on the occasions that I did leave—I returned to find my daughter sopping wet. Despite my telephone harangue to Fern, diapers were still not being changed too frequently or well.

There were other troubling signs. On a rainy day, Emma and I arrived to find the schoolroom dark. No one was in the room, and there was no note. Peering into the director's office, I found her on the phone, soliciting a new parent with glowing descriptions of the school's facilities. The facility we would have loved to find was the rainy-day room, which neither Emma nor I had ever seen—since she was sick on the two or three prior rainy days. The director finally waved her hand at me and said, "Go upstairs," so we did.

I reckoned that she meant one flight up, but no. The next floor was the wrong floor, with no one there, either. We ambled through the building, up the staircase, pausing to knock at locked stairwell doorways. I was not having a really good time, and Emma was hot under her slicker.

Finally, we found the rainy-day room, where thirty kids, most much older and bigger, were screaming at the top of their voices.

Emma's two teachers had dwindled to one. (Fern had called in sick), and that one—the one with the temper—was sitting calmly on a bench with a child, Hayley on her lap. Hayley was the only one in the class she really liked. Emma wandered around the room like a molecule. I pitied her. I felt dazed, too, in the hubbub.

Hayley and the teacher were just sitting there. No one called Emma's name. But someone came over to me and said I ought to go. "Come on, Mom, time to go," she said. And—to my shame, looking back—I went. Her tone (like that of a bartender sending a customer back to his wife) mocked me. *Mothers* have the most problems with separation, say the knowing books. And I was getting this (childless) teacher's knowing condescension.

I stood outside and tried to see Emma through the window in the door, but it was frosted. Opaque. She was in there, lost, and I was (though she didn't know it) just outside the door. And then I left.

That night, I called a child-development expert whom I know and asked her what she thought about all this. She told me, hectically, that school for two-year-olds is de facto child abuse, that she is willing to "shut that school down," if I want her to.

She told me, bluntly, that Emma could be permanently damaged from having to separate too soon.

Stammering, I tried to defend the school, Emma, myself.

"It's not the sort of school that pushes reading, you know. Or math. In fact, they're really very laid-back."

"Who cares?"

"The director was trained at Bank Street, I think."

"Bully for her! She should know better."

"A lot of the time Emma likes it," I said, continuing to play devil's advocate. "She's told me so a couple of times. Sometimes when I peer in, she's completely absorbed. Laughing, painting, squeezing great lumps of Play-Doh. I think she's getting something out of it."

"She's merely hysterical," answered the Ph.D. "Out of control. They act like they like it when they see there is no choice. But later, when she's a teenager, she'll give you hell back."

The Ultimate Threat.

"But—but I thought it would be good for her, since the new baby at home takes up so much time, and she can be with her peer group—"

I heard my source think: A-ha!

"That's the *worst* thing you can do. She feels displaced, pushed out, punished. No wonder she acts like she's happy. She thinks she did something terrible. Now she's trying to get back on your good side. She thinks you want her to like school—after all, you're practically forcing her to go. So she's pretending to like it, to please you. First step of narcissistic alienation."

The next would be as easy to trip over, I suppose.

"But the baby was born three months ago," I say, latching on to that displacement comment.

"Makes no difference. You're making a big mistake."

But what about Ilg and Ames, and "a good nursery school" being great for two-year-olds? The expert then conceded that the *occasional* two-year-old, make that a two-and-a-half-year-old girl, *might* adjust to school (and so I *still* hear from a multitude of parents), but that as a rule, you were best off not betting that that two-and-a-half-year-old girl was yours.

That night, I asked Emma if she wanted to go back to school. I told her that I loved to have her at home, and that she didn't have to go. That a lot of little kids her age didn't go to school. But that if she wanted to, that was fine, too.

She gave me her full attention as I spoke. It was one of the first times I saw her look that way: a serious, deep, almost adult expression in her eyes. I was talking to her heart of hearts, to the essence of Emma, and she said, "Want to stay home, Mommy."

"You want to stay home for now?"

"Yes. Stay home Mommy and Grabriel."

She was using the mispronunciation of her brother's name; she knows that makes me smile. But she was serious.

"Stay home, Mommy?"

"Yes, sweetie."

Good heavens, the expert was right!

After a few months, in order not to have Emma feel she'd failed something, I signed her up for a class or two at a nearby center. These were forty-five-minute fragments of the preschool experience: arts and crafts, storytime, and puzzles, running around in a padded room, etc.

Emma called the new place "play school," and liked it. She wasn't asked to separate anymore. Not being asked to separate, she was lively, cocky, and independent. All winter, no virus could touch her.

After a short time, I received a form letter from the school we'd left, part of a mass mailing for prospective parents.

"There are still spaces available at our fine school," it said. "Due to parental interest, to which we are always sensitive, we are now implementing a flexible program in which all children will be able to attend, two, three, four, or five mornings a week, depending on their needs."

Wow—even though they "adjusted better" with five?

The letter invited us to view the school, and I returned, ambivalent, to do so.

They were surprised to see me, but not unfriendly.

I looked around.

It was bittersweet seeing Emma's pictures, cotton glued to finger paint, bits of tinsel, still displayed up on the school wall. Sad to see the school go on without her. Fern seemed to be gradually loosening up; she was down on her knees, looking Hayley in the eyes. Hayley, less shy than before, was looking back and smiling. Blackie was eating straw, same as before.

Suddenly remembering that I had left a spare pair of Emma's pants in her shoebox, I went to the bathroom, where the children have their lockers. The pants were still there where I left them.

Turning to leave, I saw something new and different.

Standing sentinel on the bathroom sink was a pump bottle of Dial soap, golden, undiluted, and strong.

TWENTY-SIX

WHEREIN YOUR CHILD APPLIES TO SCHOOL

Don't get the impression, from the fact that we flew away from preschool like bats out of hell, that we didn't come squeaking right back. We all come right back, and here the metaphor changes from bats to moths, drawn toward the flame that is the New York City preschool for three-year-olds. In order to get in, you have to apply, tour, be interviewed, have your child interviewed, and—in the case of "gifted" programs—have his IQ and aptitude professionally assessed. IQ tests or not, you will pay extravagantly. Not only for tuition, but for the application itself, which tends to cost somewhere around thirty dollars. Notification arrives in the form of an envelope in March, thick if your child is accepted, thin if your child is not. Analogies to college acceptance can and should be made.

Despite the hordes of applicants, preschools tend to accept these costly petitions from September to February. Perhaps this is a major profit source for them. We, for our part, seem glad to pay, glad to tour the school with name tags taped to our lapels, glad to take our two-year-olds in to be "interviewed" for a brief quarter-hour.

We all come back, with the possible exception of mothers like

Marla. Mothers like Marla decide, somewhere in the game, that most teachers of tiny kids are neither inspired nor loving (certainly in comparison with mothers), and opt to do it—that is, keep doing it—themselves.

Marla, hip, fun, and athletic, described her three-year-old's teacher as "Miss No-No." I was familiar with Miss No-No, even though mine lived on the East Coast and Marla's on the West. After complaining to the school about this negative, easily flappable teacher, Marla learned a few things about school: 1) that she was one of the few to *ever* complain (this is an experiment in social science, intimidation subset; 2) that complaints are not universally accepted with glee (Marla was labeled a troublemaker); 3) that in most cases, mothers must vote with their feet.

Marla withdrew her active three-year-old son, and for good measure his four-year-old brother, from school. Both, she said, were delighted upon their release from No-No's domain. Were they friendless, unstimulated, subject to boredom and, worse, poor academic integration? No, no, to all the above. "They have play-dates," said Marla. "They have books, toys, art materials, fresh air. And me." As for school, "they'll get enough school after kindergarten, more than twenty years' worth, if you count college."

Mothers contemplating preschool certainly do count college. They (we) are counting it, in some sense (a sick one, usually), from the moment the child enters school at all. And for most urban mothers—this is true of New York—the operative age, if not two, is certainly three.

(By four, many urban children sit for tests administered by the Educational Records Bureau, an association of schools throughout the United States that provides standardized examinations for the pre-K crowd. Parents are told that the best preparation is a good night's sleep. A growing number, however, suspect that an even better way to prepare is via a cram course. ERB items are stolen and given to the prospective test-taker, and he/she practices, getting up to speed. Tutors in this area, as in most areas of the mother culture, stand to make a fortune. Money well spent, think the paying parents: what price Harvard?)

One mother, touring a Montessori school, asked what her three-year-old child's chances were on graduation. Meaning, she explained, "Does anyone go from here to Cambridge, Mass.?" Not directly, but still, do they go? Yes, she was told. They do. Someone had tracked down the answer to this question! Possibly, if asked, she could have provided information about Harvard Med as well.

My husband and I are, collectively, graduates of Columbia, Oxford, and Yale. So pompous are we, so sure of our brains and ability to genetically reproduce them, that we have never yet worried about whether our children would go to college in Cambridge or New Haven. Was this merely because we were sure that they would—or because we have grown beyond caring, recognizing (at last) that not all Oxbridge-Ivies are bright, good, and happy?

Too early to tell. Already we were showing dangerous signs of ambition, carefully filling in preschool applications (careful to mention the Oxford, the Yale), dressing Emma up in frocks for her interviews, shodding her in English Mary Janes (inside which one reads "by appointment to HRH Elizabeth"), which she now won't take off.

I was talking this over with an acquaintance of mine, Shana, who was saying how disgusting all this ambition is, how she, too, had been having Marla thoughts of keeping her kid home until she was five. Like me, Shana had latterly, shamefully, come to act like everyone else in town, that is, compulsive. "You just get sucked in," she confessed. "I'm disgusted with myself."

I was disgusted with her, too, for after I commiserated for a while, saying that at least we ought to find easygoing, child-centered places for our poor pressured babies, she told me that her Mimi was being interviewed for a French-speaking preschool. "Might as well go whole hog," said Shana. *"Cochon entière,"* I agreed, egging her on. "Whadya say?" asked Shana.

I was showing off my own French, all of which I learned roughly a decade after I was three. I took in culture—am still taking it in—with blood, sweat, and tears, the way culture is meant to be taken in. I was sent to ballet class (to imitate a falling leaf as well as a dying swan) before I had ever seen true ballet, and even after seeing it have little understanding of the art or why it exists.

No child should be reading Proust (or having it read to him) if the only things past that he remembers involve potty training and *pluparfait* drill at the Lycée. He should have soul, whatever that is, and soul takes a while to develop. It develops slowly. It does not like to be rushed. And no Suzuki violin or gymnastics class is going to implant the *need* to make music or move, with grace, through space and time.

Only now, for example, do I begin to understand the night flights of Bovary and Karenina, the tragedy of Lear and his two rotten daughters, the spasmodic love of Heathcliff and dead, spooky Cathy.

Dr. Elkind, too, believes that all this ballet-French lessons-violin class jazz is premature if the child has no construct for culture. Since he and I agree on this point, I am citing him. There is nothing as wonderful as an expert who backs up your gut feeling (like that child-development friend who'd told me that, at two, Emma was too young for preschool). This, I think, is the prime use of experts.

What would Elkind say, then, about "Genius" school, which (like French school to Shana) I found simultaneously attractive and abhorrent? I suspect the program is not too different from most, but the application floored me.

Examples: "Please describe your child's favorite building or art materials and the work he/she creates" or "Can your child solve problems that involve the addition of small numbers whose sums are between three and nine?" "Can your child solve problems which involve the addition of two- and three-digit numbers without carrying? For example, could your child accurately add together numbers like 126 and 33?" (Can you?)

And: "Has your child written a brief letter composed of real words to a relative or friend?" "Does he/she use appropriately in conversation words that are highly abstract and/or complex, such as 'faith,' 'sincerity' and 'grief?'" "Has your child asked the meaning of abstract words such as 'peace,' 'justice' and 'infinity'?"

These seem tall orders for the two-year-old; the application, politely, allows you to answer "not yet," instead of the blunter "God, no!"

I must add, however, that Emma *did do some* of the geniusy things. She made up word games, laughed at puns, knew her colors, could sing "Twinkle Twinkle," and appropriately used such abstract concepts as "burned out." (Just kidding.) As I held on to the application (and as she aged), she began to reveal more and more of its desiderata, and I had a chance to warp into the would-be stage mother. I began to think, hmmm. What a burden, the gifted child. I shall try to keep her as happy as possible, with friends her own age and lots of oatmeal-raisin cookies—as she goes to MIT!

It was a lot like the time I was stopped in the park by a modeling agent. The woman was jogging one way, Emma and I were strolling the

other, when the agent doubled back and jogged in place, staring, nod-
ding, at my pretty child. "A blonde-blue!" she shouted. "Call me!" After
shoving a card into my hand, she was off again, and running.

I thought about it for a moment. Not the money. The pride, the
vanity. It made me feel good to realize that I had produced a visual
winner, someone who had "it." After the moment passed, however, I felt
sick about the notion of looks counting in childhood (it's bad enough
that they do in adulthood), that other children, the brown-eyed, the
short, would be passed by on the agent's jog.

I was repelled, too, by the notion of selling any aspect of my
daughter's appeal. If she was pretty, fine; did I (we) have to cash that
in? That thought was coming back to me as I contemplated the question
of my little girl's purported "genius." Did we have to trumpet every
God-given aspect of my daughter's being? Did we have to sell it in the
marketplace? Three jumps through the hoop will get you into the gifted
program; from there you can write your own ticket. Except that it won't
be your own.

In the course of my work, I have attended modeling interviews
at children's magazines. Toddlers are tarted up in huge glasses and
baseball caps (askew), babies are kept from sliming themselves by the
withholding of a lunchtime feed, infants are kept awake in a small,
hot room, etc.

When asked why they do it, few people mention money; there isn't
much in print journalism anyway. (One child made about sixty-five dollars in one shoot; the mother had gone around for days, and the final
photo was in a magazine she couldn't find and was never sent.) For most
parents, according to one fashion coordinator, the true motives include
the filling of time (once spent, perhaps, in pursuit of a career), and the
fulfillment of a need to be important, wanted (once satisfied, perhaps,
by the pursuit of a career). "I wouldn't want this for my kid," is the
common refrain heard among professionals.

Given the choice, I didn't want this for my kid. I love Emma and
her smashing brother too much to sell them, feature by feature, whether
it be eyes, the shadowy cleft of a chin, or the ability to solve a family
problem or create a family pun. Taken out of context and sold for status,
these intimate gifts of beauty and brains become the Elephant Man's
bones, unindicative of his greater soul. So back I turned to the normal,
the average, the loving, the fun. School, I mean. I turned to the sort

usually termed "developmental," that is, the sort attuned to the child, and not to letters, numbers, or the history of feudal Europe.

In a "normal" preschool, ideally, the child's own temperament is allowed to develop. His love of play (call it work, or learning, if it soothes your conscience) is encouraged, and he can learn, in unthreatening circumstances, to be with others, to cooperate, and to share.

My daughter seemed to crave the company of others, more so since she had stopped going to the two-year-olds' preschool. She still kept chasing all those day-care kids all over the park, still yelling "friends, friends!" Still lusting after their juice and crackers.

That expert friend who thought it was child abuse to have kids go to school at two thought it was fine at three. (What a difference a year makes, she said. She is right.) So we applied. As I have been explaining, however, one needs to go through this odd process a year in advance. At two.

In order to spare her the trauma, if any, of going through any more "rejection" or "failure"—an inherent part of this barbaric process—I take Emma to her first interview under the guise of its being a play-date of sorts. I say, "Emma, we're going to a fun school to play with some toys with a big friend."

"Fun school," to distinguish it from the not-so-fun school she'd already attended.

"Some toys" equal Montessori materials. The particular school in question was about as Montessori as you could get without inducing a nervous breakdown. Every toy had a purpose. Every question had an answer. When we went for the tour (sans Emma), all my husband and I could see was a sea of heads, quiet, assiduously doing their "work." One girl was washing a chair, which made me laugh. (Points off!)

I laugh again, more privately, at another Montessori school when I see this plaque in the bathroom:

STAFF MUST WASH HANDS BEFORE RETURNING TO WORK . . . PLEASE.
—Maria Montessori
The Montessori Method
(1912)

Mistakenly, I had always attributed that quote to "Anonymous." Apparently, mine was the only laughter in the Montessori system that day—I was a screwball on the loose. Everyone else, the parents, the headmistress, and certainly the children, knew what Montessori was all about.

Basically, it's about focusing on what interests you, sitting quietly on a mat to do it, learning practically and sensually (through touch) about life, and doing those darned endless puzzles: little pegs into little boards forevermore. You learn to count through rosarylike beads, to polish pennies, to pour water, to do an elaborate map of Africa, to go on to Harvard, from what I could tell, and certainly to sponge the hell out of a child's chair.

Significantly, Dr. Elkind—and many others—have only good to say about Montessori. My husband and my wonderful cousin, who may be the best mother I know, adore it.

But I feel rocky. It's so quiet here, I think. Why aren't they talking to each other? Why aren't they laughing? Why do I feel like *I'm* the one who'll make the next noise?

And why are they polishing those pennies? Don't they have anything better to do? (You can see why teachers love me.)

Hiding my name tag, I ask why there are no dolls, no fireman hats, no big fake stove. "We have no fantasy here," says the headmistress. Is her name Mrs. Gradgrind, same as the name of a fictional, or fantasy, character by a soulful chap called Dickens? No, it is some other name, but the song is the same. Facts, facts, facts.

"You can fantasize at home," she adds, somewhat pityingly. I think (half-fantasizing already): Okay then, I *will!* (Here is the first sign that we will be receiving the slim envelope and not the fat.)

As we talked afterward in a nearby coffee shop, my husband, unrepelled, says that here is freedom. Then why is it so infernally quiet? I say, raising my voice. It is quiet because of the quiet of free choice, concentration, depth of purpose, says he. Here is—he hopes—a place where children choose what they want to do (so long, I say, as they choose to do those infernal puzzles and penny-shinings). They did all seem happy, I admit, though I had thoughts of Stepford wives and pod people (and they, too, seemed so happy). My husband tells me that schools like this are normal throughout Europe. Indeed, Montessori is held in the highest regard on the Continent. (But didn't the Continent give us Fascism and "I am following no dark, Semitic, feminine fantasies, but humorlessly polishing pennies—I mean, following orders?")

Though informal, warm, and unclassifiable himself, Paul likes the polished, English look of the school. It is in a stone church; it looks, as Emma later tells me, like a castle; it is incredibly well endowed with space, light, toys, those Montessori materials, and some serious-looking teachers.

"Big friend": This is my wildly inaccurate appellation for the Montessori teacher Emma and I are about to meet for our interview.

TWENTY-SEVEN

INTERVIEW HELL

L et us begin with the interrupted nap on the day of the Big Interview. Let us begin with the wild, electric hair on Emma's head as she wakes from her abruptly disturbed nap.

I look at my child's fine blond hair and realize it has never looked so electrified before. Her bangs, all one thousand individual hairs of her bangs, are dancing on end; the rest of the coiffure looks like a wheat field after a tornado.

Animal instinct kicks in, and I begin moussing her with my own saliva, a Labrador lapping her pup. Emma alternately groans with half-sleep and giggles. Poor thing, she is tickled that I am about to take her on an adventure, a play-date in a fun school with a big friend. All this in the middle of her sacrosanct (to me) naptime. Poor thing, being curious; it would only hurt her in the end.

We get there on time, but the teacher is late. This gives Emma the time to discover the assembly room, with the stage covered with both Christmas trees and Hanukkah dreidels, or as Emma puts it, "all kinds triangles, Mommy!" Charming child, you know your geometric shapes; this will come in handy, I hope.

Emma begins to climb the stage despite my admonition. She begins to pick up a long strand of tinsel despite my admonition.

At all times, fill in "despite my admonition," and fill in that Emma is having a ball.

Uh-oh. Here comes Big Friend.

"Could you—I'm afraid she can't—"

"I know, I'm just getting her down."

Big Friend to Emma: "You need to get off that stage."

Note: I hate that "need to" locution. It means "have to," and we all know it. Anyway, Emma ignores Big Friend and addresses me.

"I—Mommy—I jump down these big stairs, okay?"

"NO!!" (The teacher, in an uncharacteristic—I think—moment of uncontrolled emotion.)

Emma then walks down the stairs quite nicely. She follows the teacher into one of those beautifully endowed classrooms and sets out to have herself a field day.

Big Friend pulls out a little blue chair at the far end.

"Emma, you need to sit here."

"Mommy, come, too!"

The cry that rips my heart out. I waver.

I remember the times that I left her at school, when she didn't feel sure of herself, the time when she walked into that rainy-day room she'd never seen, to the teacher who didn't like her (who'd held another child on her lap and didn't get up), searching for the teacher she liked better (who was absent), and overwhelmed by the number and volume of kids she'd never met, all having rainy-day gym. She asked me to stay. And I'd wavered—and gone.

Or the time when, lying on the changing table, the first time I'd left her, Emma saw me return and said "Go away" in her dullest voice, and both teachers took that to mean she had adjusted well and simply wanted me to go (she could fend for herself), and I'd protested that she was angry, that she said "Go away" at home only when I'd finish nursing Gabriel. But they just stared me down, so I went.

And now, the teacher, more distinguished, more stern, and more sure than any I'd ever met, is telling me to go. And this time it's not even remotely for the good of my child, but because that is how the test gets carried on. A convenience for them. Step One of test, perhaps.

And therefore graded.

I don't know what to do. Remember, experts had said, and—more important—I *believed,* that two-year-olds don't like to be placed alone with strangers. That they shouldn't have to "separate" if they don't want to. And why, under the circumstances, should Emma suddenly want to?

I feel a pain in my gut. The teacher has not made the slightest eye contact with my child. She has not really looked at her. Emma always seems to sense who is a true friend. Big Friend is not a true friend. We both know it.

I listen to Emma, again. She is clear about this whole thing.

"Mommy, stay here, too."

Am I going to hurt my child—even for a few minutes—for the sake of an order from an impersonal source? A thought flashes into my mind: Any school that makes a child plead "Mommy, stay," for the sake of an interview does not like or care about children. What it likes is itself, what it cares about is itself and its rigid rules. I think the technical term for this is lack of child-centeredness.

I stand there and say, "Look, I know this child, and she will be more comfortable"—like any two-year-old—"if I do stay."

I get a cold look for that. And, I'm sure, a bad mark.

The interview begins.

"Emma sit down."

For Emma is up, coming around to my side.

I ask her to sit down, and tell her that I won't leave. I'm standing right behind her, and even though she can't see me, I can see everything. (If I couldn't, I wouldn't be able to report the following.)

Emma makes an attempt at contact with the teacher. It isn't easy. The woman is formal, trained, polished. Emma gives her the thundering wet raspberry that is her current calling card. A patient pause.

Then the teacher takes out three cloth bags. She lays them on the table.

"Emma, here are three bags. I am going to open the first one and show you what is inside."

She opens the bag and takes out a blue block. The block is square.

At home, Emma has wooden blocks, plastic blocks, foam blocks, pegs, cylinder, Legos. She builds huge, Emma-sized towers with blocks. Improbable things. Mansions.

The teacher takes out another square block. This one is green.

"Emma, I am going to ask you to make a tower of two blocks."

Big deal, thinks Emma. She is after the bag, the entire bag. The teacher is boring, the blocks are not; she wants them.

"Emma, you need to listen to me."

The restraining hand is on Emma's reaching hand. It prevails. The lesson continues. The teacher carefully places the blue block on top of the green block. She clears her throat. She speaks:

"Emma, this is a tower of two blocks. I am showing you something, Emma. Are you listening? You need to look and to listen.

"What color is the top block?"

Emma knows all the colors. She has known them for over a year. When I first showed her red, on a ground of white, she asked me to name the color of the ground. I told her "white." Now, like a house-painter, she can distinguish shades of red, shades of white. Of course, she can distinguish dark blue from light ("Daddy's eyes darker than Emma's"). She tells me what a color is when I'm not sure. I say, is this tomato red? She says, "Some red, a little bit orange." Did I say house-painter? She is like a color consultant, my sharp-eyed Emma.

"What color is the top block, Emma?"

Emma pauses and says, "Purple."

Not only is the teacher not amused, she must think Emma is color-blind, ignorant, and—far worse—eccentric. The one possibility the expert does not consider is that Emma is trying to be funny and break the ice. (Emma does not consider that the ice may have been frozen for years.)

When asked about the green block, Emma says, "Red?"

The blocks are put back into their cloth bag.

At that point, I protest that Emma is my master builder and trusty color consultant, but am not believed. I have an impulse to take Emma by the hand and say something damning and final about the school, its methods, this teacher, and life. I control myself, but am seething with love and hate. Love for my child, hatred for the one who isn't in on this, and doesn't *want* in on this.

There is nothing more infuriating than not being believed about, not being considered an authority on, your own child.

A further demerit is added, I suppose. Not only have I not followed orders about leaving the room, apparently I have not realized that I need to be silent.

After scarcely a pause (time is passing), the second bag is opened. Little dolls spill out. These are not playful-looking dolls. They are clinical, made of hard rubber, and represent the members of some theoretical family in which father is tall, with a glossy plastic head of black hair, mother is fair, skirted, and thin, and brother and sister, towheads, the latter in pigtails and a dress. There is also a baby in a hard plastic baby bonnet.

As with the blocks, I suppose Emma will ace this one handily. She has a set of Fisher-Price Little People that includes father, mother, baby brother, Emma herself, and several friends of both sexes. In both this clinical family and the Fisher-Price one, the little girl bears a cliché resemblance to Emma herself, and she knows it.

The teacher isolates the girl doll.

"Emma, is this a girl or a boy?"

Emma looks at her with wonderment. She says it's a boy.

At this point, I begin to resent her a little. Come on, kid, I think; you're making me look bad. It took that long, it always does, and I feel disloyal. I keep my mouth shut this time. The teacher repeats the question, and Emma concedes that it is, in fact, a girl.

"Good.

"What is her name?"

"Emma."

Emma calls many of her toys "Emma." When she first came in, she was carrying a small plush dinosaur (and yes, she knows what a dinosaur is, and a whale, shark, and jellyfish, dammit). Teacher asked her what the name of the creature was. Emma said "Emma." She thinks it's a great name. (Though lately, she has started to call everything either "Boodle," Mackie," or "Jammo.")

"No, Emma. That is *your* name."

Emma giggles. Teacher does not. Game over. The rubber girl doll is put back into the bag. The baby doll is proffered.

"What's this?"

"Gabriel!"

Here, I inject the fact that that is the name of Emma's little brother. The teacher looks relieved that Emma has not had a vision of angels.

She shows Emma the father doll.

"Daddy!"

My brilliant Emma is on a roll here.

"And what is your daddy's name?"

Come on, Emma, tell her "Paul," the way you say it at home, when we laugh and chide you, or "honey," or "puffins." You know everything, dammit, why don't you perform???!

Emma says, "Emma."

The family dolls are put back into their bag.

The third bag is proffered.

"Guess what I have in here, Emma?"

Emma, bless her, is still ready for the day to pick up. I am a deep crimson color by now, a blue-red, as Emma would call it. "Sonia," she would say, in that same impetuous mood that makes her call Daddy "Paul," "you—you blue-red in your cheeks now."

The third bag had balls. Of course she'll (we'll?) ace this one. Emma loves running, catching, jumping. She is intrepid and fit. She is agile and quick. And we play ball all the time.

Teacher takes out a tennis ball and says:

"Emma. I am going to rrroooooollll the ball to you. And I want you to rrooooolll it back to me."

Emma is delighted. As soon as the ball is rolled to her, she grabs it, and—running over to me—tosses it a short distance, into my hands.

"Mommy, let's play ball!"

Teacher, not that I blame her, gives me a look. I rrrrooooolll the ball to her, and she rrrooooollls it to Emma.

Emma grabs it, and—running over to me—tosses it a short distance, into my hands.

The Grimm-Shakespearean bit with three bags is now ended. Teacher leads Emma toward the door, stopping—or is it Emma who stops?—before a set of bells. Emma takes the stick ("It's called a 'striker,'" says the teacher, "Can you say 'striker'?") and begins to play a few notes. At home, need I say, she has seen, plucked, blown, or thumped upon a drum, a tambourine, a guitar, a mandolin, a kazoo, several horns, and a digitally sampled piano that turns, at the touch of a button (which she has touched) into an organ, celesta, clavichord, etc. She also has a set of musical bells and a book with a tiny piano built in, which she plays in bed, at night (*into* the night). So our Emma knows from music, okay?

The teacher (is this getting to be an old story?) wants her to play the bells in a certain way, in a certain order. She also, still, wants Emma to say "striker." Emma plays a few more notes, then decides to move the bells to a different table. Her favorite pastime is systematic re-arrangement, not, unfortunately, on this Montessori syllabus. This having been accomplished (the teacher has given up), my child turns to address the fish in the nearby aquarium.

"Fish," she says. "You have mouths. You should eat your food and you should talk, but—but don't eat and talk same time, okay, fish? You could choke, fish, so be careful." As an afterthought, she adds, "Want a lollipop, too? I have a cherry lollipop, could share it."

She says all this to the fish, and the teacher is listening, baffled. She turns to me and says, somewhat pityingly, "You know, in a year or so, you'll be surprised; she'll really acquire language skills. When they can talk, they really do blossom."

Apparently, the teacher has not understood a word my genius has said. I am outraged that she has found all these meaningful, funny words a mere hodgepodge of nonsense. I am amazed that she has found my meaningful, funny child a mere hodgepodge of nonsensical impulse. Again, I protest.

"She's talking. She *is* talking. Language skills? She had about two hundred words in her vocabulary at about fifteen months. I know because I couldn't believe it, so I counted. (Okay, it was compulsive, but I'm a writer.) And she's just told the fish a little story. In paragraph form. With elements of fantasy, and kindness."

"Well," says the teacher, "*I* didn't get it."

No, she didn't.

The teacher then abruptly turned to Emma and said, "You have to go now."

Emma: "No, like to play."

Me: "At her age, isn't it better to give a better, I don't know, transition? Like, 'We have to go in a minute'?"

That last bit of unsolicited maternal brilliance is borrowed, as it happens, from Stanley Turecki's book on the "difficult" child. That book has proved invaluable. It not only helped me realize that Emma was not difficult but gave me tips to prevent her seeming so. Tips like not interrupting her without warning.

Teacher: "We need the classroom. Now."

I drag Emma out, and, of course, she looks upset. She turns back to the classroom and finally meets the teacher's eye. Something she sees makes her wobble. She falls to the floor, legs splayed, working herself up to a real cry. Then she stops herself, changes mood, and looks up challengingly. She's having a sort of perverse fun, now. A tantrum may be in the offing.

I look at the teacher, and I look at my child, sprawled open-legged on the spotless floor. All I can say, and it makes me laugh, is: "So is this what you're looking for?"

Later, we sit in a pizzeria, girl to girl. Emma chews seriously. She does not talk. Neither do I. From time to time, I wipe her mouth. From time to time, she wipes her mouth. She takes large, thirsty swigs of water. We are two tired athletes, both slightly winded.

I feel intensely close to her.

Still later, at one of Emma's "gym" classes, I ask a father I know (it's Sunday morning) how his daughter did at this particular school interview. I know that he likes the school very much (I am beginning to hold that against him). And I know that his daughter, Alice, is somber and shy. I am looking for confirmation that she, too, did not want her mother to leave, that she, too, talked incoherently to a tankful of fish. But no.

Alice has done great, he tells me. She walked right off, into the classroom with the teacher. She came out after exactly fifteen minutes. The father, of course, did not see what had happened in there. He did not know the mystery of the three bags. He only knew that the teacher said of Alice, "I'd love to have her in my class."

Hmm. This raises competitive issues in my mind. I still say (privately) screw 'em. But the ambitious side has been summoned in me, and I think, let's all meet up in, oh, twenty years, and see who's got the Nobel (or novel), shall we?

Now, Emma is almost four. She goes to a school where the teachers are patient, loving, happy, and experienced. (And both of them have children of their own.) They seem to see my daughter as she is. They like her. She likes them, and loves her new friends. I am proud of her. She is proud of herself. On play-dates, she greets them at the elevator, laughing, saying, "Come to my home! I have cats! You can pet them! I will read for you!" She mothers them exuberantly. (She has had much experience with the now rambunctious, mischievous Gabriel.) Emma has claimed one special friend for now, a whimsical sprite I'll call Teddy.

One day, as I walk her away from school, Emma remembers that she had wanted to tell Teddy something. She wants to go back to the lobby and find him. By the time she tells me this, we have walked a long block away from that lobby. Emma has stopped to have some cornballs. She has drained a juice box, and she has stared at a big black dog. I am pretty sure that Teddy will no longer be where we last saw him, greeting his mother.

Still, after thinking about it, I take Emma's hand and we turn around. She seems to need to *see* that he's gone. So we walk back to school, at a half run actually, to find Teddy.

As we hurry, Emma looks up at me. She stops in her tracks, as though she had never seen me before.

"I have a secret for *you*," she says.

Every night, before she and Gabriel go to sleep, I tell them this secret: "I love you." Gabriel then leaps up to squeeze me; sometimes he rubs my nose with his. Emma tends to smile into her pillow, suddenly shy. "Don't go, then," she'll say. "Stay forever."

"I love you" is what I expect her to say now. Isn't it obvious?

"I chose the best mommy" is what she does say, ever original. She is never obvious. No test can quantify her, and I love her for it. I chose the best daughter, and son. Paul and I are still wondering how—despite all the struggles—we got so lucky in love.

Not that I mean to brag.

Well, yes, I do.

TWENTY-EIGHT

CONCLUSION: WHEREIN YOU'RE ON YOUR OWN

*T*here seems a paradox in buying a book about motherhood that tells you to go easy on those motherhood books. In a way, it's a hair-of-the-dog cure. Makes you feel good, puts some fire in your belly—but eventually you'll have to throw those bottles out. I am thinking not only of this book, but of several by David Elkind, for instance. He was certainly an influence on me. Had it not been for him, I'd have taken genius-makers like Susan Ludlington-Hoe and Glenn Doman all the more seriously. T. Berry Brazelton, I think, was the one who reassured me that cold-turkeying the pacifier or bottle was (as I suspected) a rather cruel thing to force a child to do. And Louise Bates Ames and Francis Ilg, countering the Mother-can-never-be-replaced line, assured me that baby-sitters can and should be sought out for relief. There are always experts who suit your line of thought, gadgets and tapes that buoy you up. But having used them all, we must build huge bonfires, sit by the warmth, and plan our own lives, propless.

In writing this book, I have made the assumption that its readers are inundated by mother culture. I have supposed that simply by being parents, they have been exposed to busy arguments, pro and con, about every aspect of child-rearing, and that they're lost in the dense, small-printed wasteland. In the course of writing *Mothering Heights*, however, I have met a few parents who could actually have used a parenting course (one was biting her child's bottom to stop him from biting her shoulder, another was pleading with her four-year-old daughter to "stop torturing" her).

I have, also, met a few kids who needed to go to Gymboree (they lived in small apartments with their parents, dogs, and canaries). I have met the odd person who actually *should* have thought twice about having babies so closely spaced together (me). And I have met many who needed, and consulted with, a child psychologist. So let it not be said that an expert or two isn't handy at times, or critical.

But surrender your mind to them? No.

We could use a few more skeptics in our midst. Good mothers and fathers are still dragging reluctant (or falsely eager) little ones to improvement programs, buying magazines with names like *Smart Child*, and signing their fetuses up for French lessons. They seem not to realize that the best, the only real, improvement program for the small child is at home, and I don't mean flash cards. I mean you.

As a friend of mine said, "Better to read Austen than Leach." As I say, better to read *Zen and the Art of Motorcycle Maintenance* than anything about motorcycle maintenance, or child maintenance. Those who can, do. Those who can't, teach themselves by doing.

Our children know this. They are there to teach us a thing or two about who they are as people. If we want to, we can see them, unblocked by mounds of paper, ink, and fancy plastic toys. They are the little stars that twinkle in the sky, the ones that illuminate the path for us travelers. How does that poem go?

> Then the traveler in the dark
> Thanks you for your tiny spark
> He would not know which way to go
> If you did not twinkle so.

If my children did not twinkle so, I'm sure I would not have learned to be more patient, to hold my tongue, to be kinder, to let things be. I can wait for years (I'm going to have to) for a good vacation. Put it this way: I am in the process of reinterpreting what a good vacation is, what free time is, and how an adult regroups and grows.

Here is the paradox: What children take from us, they give. When we are not totally "free," we learn how to cope with a smaller world, less time, less luxury (getting up late and staying up late used to be mine). We become people who feel more deeply, question more deeply, hurt much more deeply, and love more deeply.

We are growing people here, young and old.

Sort of the thrill we wanted when, in the extremes of young fancy, we hoped our lives would be rich, romantic, and complex. We've got that now, at home. No chance to run, no need to flee. We're inside now, and it's all here: the depths, and the greatest heights.

TWENTY-NINE

INCONCLUSION: Q AND A FOR PARENTS AND EXPERTS

A little advice is a dangerous thing. For every expert who tells you about vacations in Grenada causing irreparable harm, there is another who tells you to take time off, for your marriage is the basis of all childbearing, and you should be sexily selfish on a regular basis.

I have attempted to provide a few simple questions on issues so primitive as to be laughable—unless they are yours. (They seem to be everybody's.)

See what was asked, what was answered, and what this mother found through the best teacher of all. Parenthood, that existentialist front.

1. The pacifier question:

Should you use one, knowing that it will help your child sleep, not cry in the middle of a restaurant, adjust to the cold, cruel world, satisfy his orality?

Answer: Oh definitely, say the experts. They're great. They actually pacify. (In England, they are called "soothers," though they used to be called "dummies.") Baby needs to suck. Of course, you will be careful not to "overuse" them: For instance, if your baby is splattered and basted in baby turd and urine, you will not reach the conclusion that he can and should be easily pacified. Nor should they be used for "too long." At some point, usually when the child seems to be thoroughly addicted, you should try to wean him.

At that point, say I, you are more than back to square one, as the baby's habits are stronger, his cry longer, and strangers' unwanted staring more pointed. See what you think the next time you see a "plugged-up" toddler. "Oh that mother," you'll say, "and oh that immature child! Can't she pull that thing out of his mouth!"

Well, just try.

Other experts, perhaps sensing this fate, say, Don't start with pacifiers. Try instead to lead them to their thumbs, which are always, as Brazelton points out, at the ends of their hands. But watch that they don't become addicted to their thumbs, as you will face the same public ignominy faced by the pacifier crew.

Members of that crew, we gleefully gave the pacifier to our first child, marveling at its magic. (The effect of this small bit of rubber on an overwrought child causes much addiction in the parent.)

Over the course of a year or more, we managed to lose a few hundred pacifiers; we always bought more to stock up. Having several around the home made us feel safe, rich, immune to chaos. Especially at night: There is an awful stage where you have to sow the baby's crib with pacifiers, hoping that if she gets up, she'll find one before the first shriek tears from her throat.

Eventually, thinking we noticed an incipient overbite, we tried to wean our child from the pacifier. No dice. We tried letting her have a bottle of water in bed. Wishfully, we thought she'd drink the water, lay the bottle down, and sleep. But no. She grew addicted to the bottle, day and night, indulgently chuckling at our growing collection of appealing cups (some spouted, some straw-bearing, some plain).

Our public shame merely increased.

Nevertheless, with our second child, we turned immediately to the pacifier. Better that, we said, than to wake Emma up with the comfortless cries of her brother. And, after all, some of the experts are all for it.

2. The television question:

Should you turn it on, knowing that it will give you a moment's peace, *and* that certain high-quality fare is available, both on the educational channel and on tape? Or should you be stoical and false, disdaining the tube that you yourself (admit it) are addicted to?

Answer: Never turn that box on. Experts (Marie Winn, author of *The Plug-in Drug,* foremost among them) are positive that to do so will alter your child's ability to be fully human. They are opposed to television in any form. They feel that the set itself hypnotizes the viewer, that the child will inevitably exercise less, think less, watch more, eat more, and be more of an openmouthed idiot.

They even feel this way about *Sesame Street,* so there is no arguing with these experts.

Yes, of course, in moderation, say the other experts. Turn to them, knowing that with supervision and limit-setting, the television can be an enriching experience, a living mobile, an educational tool. This team neglects to mention the little miniholiday that the boob tube is for the parents, but piety is, sadly, the name of the child-rearing game.

In my own case, I opted of course for the set, which I limited to PBS and videos of quality, no commercial TV at all (I can't stand the ads), and a limit of about an hour and a half a day.

Note the suspect use of the word "about." For any child is bound to want more and more. And mine did. (Even the little one sits mesmerized before tapes that I bought—I *think*—only to write about.) Now they both beg for more, and it is only through the most elaborate ruses that I manage to convince them that real, 3-D life is a pleasant alternative.

Sometimes I turn the thing off, discovering to my mixed pleasure and horror that they have not even noticed.

3. Should a mother work, or should she stay home?

Answer: Oh, she should definitely work, say some experts. Children of mothers who work are resourceful, personable, and clever. (Several studies place them ahead of their peers, if you're keeping score.) Resourceful, too, are their mothers, who offer most wonderful role models. And, of course, these children are likely to be treated less resentfully by their fulfilled moms, who have it all: kids, fulfillment, a paycheck, and a host of vague physiological symptoms that won't go away.

Oh, she should definitely not work, say others, who have found profound emotional deprivation and repressed anger in the children of mothers who work. These experts feel that a woman should stay home at least until her child is three. This is especially difficult when you consider that some of them also feel that children should be spaced three years apart.

Everyone seems to forget that some mothers must work, not only for financial reasons, but because they would go crazy at home, thus treating their children to undesirable visions of boredom and rage.

4. How many children should you have, and how many years apart should they be spaced?

Answer: Some of you may realize what a personal matter this question is, and hope against hope that no expert would dare take parental prerogative away and actually answer it.

But no.

Some experts think that no child will be happy unless spaced at least three years away from the nearest sibling, and for those of us no longer in our twenties, that seems to foreclose the question of how many siblings there will ultimately be. They argue that the first three years of life must be spent in an untrammeled paradise, together with Mommy, or else the child will face some sort of developmental/emotional harm, as well as possible permanent antagonism to family members—especially the ones who trammeled some vital bits of the above paradise. (I must confess, though, that there is something to be said—from the point of view of the *parent*—for having one child out of diapers, in preschool, and relatively benign before you spring for the second.)

More lenient scholars, the lovely Brazelton among them, say, essentially, do what you can, and what makes you happy; the rest is commentary.

Some popular advice-givers I've read mention that larger families cause greater numbers of divorce (Dr. Joyce Brothers), and even suggest that one consider adoption before choosing to have more than two children (Dear Abby). This latter would come as unwelcome wisdom to my own literary agent, a wonderful mother whose fourth child will soon be celebrating his first birthday.

5. *If your small child keeps getting up at night, how should you handle it?*

Answer: It takes less time to go in and deal with it than to wait for the child to settle, say some. Penelope Leach has actually drawn a graph proving (she thinks) that it is more sensible, in the long run, to just get up and see what the kid wants.

No, you should stay in bed, say the other experts (led by the famous Dr. Richard Ferber, author of the tantalizingly titled *Solve Your Child's Sleep Problems*). You stay put, gradually teaching the child how to settle himself. Otherwise, you'll end up getting up and down all night long. Soon you will become psychopathic.

Some mothers martyr themselves, others note. They have the child in bed with them, they rock the child all night, nurse all night, etc.

And you know what La Leche would say about that. Do it! Do it more! Do it forever!

I tend to favor the let-them-learn-to-sleep routine, provided it works. Luckily, in my house, it did.

6. *Speaking of martyrs, should you become one, if only to forever stop the pounding waves of guilt?*

Answer: Depending on the vintage of your experts, you should and should not.

Some experts demand that you do everything with the child in mind. Space them three years apart, never work, get up for every squeak, nurse until the SATs, etc.

Others allow you to have a life as well as a child, believing that a happy, fulfilled person is bound to be a better parent.

(Although sometimes one confuses their happiness with our own.)

As this question of how much I must give continues to eat at me (I never feel I can do enough), I will let my hairdresser, Donna, have the final word.

Seeing my anguish, one day, when I said, "I wish I were home now; Emma needs me; I never do enough for her; I wish she could see my love; I wish she were always happy; I wish she and Gabriel got along perfectly; I wish I had never caused either of them any pain; I wish I could let them devour my breast as the legendary pelican is said to do; I wish—"

Donna kindly cut me off and said, "For God's sake, no one who worries as much as you do could be a really bad mother!"

A reasonable paraphrase of Bettelheim, that.

And she said, "If you do more for your kids than you want to, if you resent them, *then* they'll suffer. Set your life up, what you can stand, what you can't, what you can take, what you can't. Don't force your moods all day (only sometimes). Don't put your phony grin on. Don't swallow anger. Don't take abuse. That way you'll enjoy yourself better. You'll be clear in what you convey. And the rest, what you can do, will be full, rich and genuine. Kids can tell when you're really giving something, because the pleasure will show in your face. That's what they'll see: How much you enjoy them, how much you love being their parent."

As Donna spoke, she gave me a really short haircut that I am still growing out. It will grow out in time.

Donna has no kids yet, but her advice hit me where I live. And that is the best basis on which to agree with any expert.

LIBRARY WESTERN IOWA TECH COMM COLLEGE

9 3567 00055 5937